PRAIS

—The Beginner's Guide to
**Signs, Wonders and
the Supernatural Life**

James has written a wonderful book for every person, from every walk of life, to be taught how to live a supernatural life in a natural way. He does it in such a biblical and balanced way that it should be must reading for every new believer. I highly recommend this great gift to the Body of Christ.

Ché Ahn
President of Harvest International Ministries
Sr. Pastor, Harvest Rock Church

In some ways, we are living in a "post-charismatic movement" era. The move of the Spirit has become so ordinary in some circles that we no longer press in to the fullness of all that God desires. Not so for James Goll. Even while mourning the death of his wife, Michal Ann, and battling against medical prognoses, James does not give in or give up. *The Beginner's Guide to Signs, Wonders and the Supernatural Life* is profound in its simplicity, clarity and passion. It challenges those of us who have not yet experienced the fullness of the Spirit while confronting those of us who have been here for a while. If you want more of God, this book will help you "be at home in the supernatural life." If you have become comfortable, the book can shake you awake.

Don Finto
Author, *Your People Shall Be My People* and
God's Promise and the Future of Israel

We are entering the most supernatural season that we have known in the last four generations. *The Beginner's Guide to Signs, Wonders and the Supernatural Life* is a wonderful tool for anyone who is pressing into revelation to live his or her life on this earth as Jesus did. James Goll lays a strong foundation and acknowledges the supernatural abilities that are available to the believer. This is our birthright given by the Great Exchange that Jesus purchased for us at Calvary. James introduces us to the Person of the Holy Spirit as the power of witness for God's supernatural character and our God-infused life. He also brings a valid balance to living in this supernatural realm and reminds us that the only wineskin that can hold this Precious Wine is one that has developed a Christ-like character. Read this book and get prepared for supernatural encounters!

Chuck D. Pierce
President, Global Spheres Inc.
President, Glory of Zion International
Harvest Watchman, Global Harvest

In *The Beginner's Guide to Signs, Wonders and the Supernatural Life*, James Goll has done a masterful job in making the supernatural natural. This book will activate the power of the Holy Spirit within you and will raise your faith level of expectation to see God do the miraculous in and through you. Thank you, James, for this empowering word that will release the Body of Christ into the fullness of our purpose and destiny to experience and demonstrate the kingdom of God.

Jane Hamon
Author of the bestseller *Dreams and Visions*

James Goll is one of those gifted people who has the ability to take the sublime and often lofty perception of the spiritual realm and put it in terms that anyone can grasp and apply to his or her own life. For that reason, his new book *The Beginner's Guide to Signs, Wonders and the Supernatural Life* is a great resource for living this natural life in the most supernatural way possible!

Jane Hansen Hoyt
President/CEO, Aglow International

Are you tired of trying to live the life you really want to live, but continually coming up short? Well, this book will help you turn the corner. James Goll has given us a simple, uncomplicated guidebook that will take you step by step down the pathway toward a life that is naturally supernatural. You will love this book!

C. Peter Wagner
Chancellor, Wagner Leadership Institute

The Beginner's Guide to Signs, Wonders and the Supernatural Life is a must-read for every believer! Jim takes the mystery out of supernatural life and makes it practical and achievable. Believers need this book in an hour when many are hungry for life outside the religious box of tradition! I highly recommend this book for all those who desire to live in the fullness of life that Jesus purchased for them!

Barbara Wentroble
President of International Breakthrough Ministries
Author of *Prophetic Intercession; Praying with Authority; Rise to Your Destiny, Woman of God* and *Removing the Veil of Deception*

James Goll has written another winner. In *The Beginners Guide to Signs, Wonders and the Supernatural Life*, he writes both from the perspective of the Word and the Spirit as well as from character and anointing. And he didn't forget to prepare us so we could jump off the cliff and start releasing the supernatural. This is a great discipling book that came out of James's life and experience. I am going to use this book myself with beginners.

Barbara J. Yoder
Senior Pastor and Lead Apostle, Shekinah Christian Church
Founder and Apostolic Leader, Breakthrough Apostolic Ministries Network

Signs, Wonders and
The Supernatural Life

JAMES W. GOLL

Regal

From Gospel Light
Ventura, California, U.S.A.

Published by Regal
From Gospel Light
Ventura, California, U.S.A.
www.regalbooks.com
Printed in the U.S.A.

Library of Congress Cataloging-in-Publication Data
Goll, Jim W.
The beginner's guide to signs, wonders, and the supernatural life / James W. Goll.
p. cm.
Includes bibliographical references (p.   ).
ISBN 978-0-8307-5138-9 (trade paper)
1. Christian life—Pentecostal authors. 2. Supernatural (Theology)
3. Holy Spirit. I. Title.
BV4509.5.G62 2010
248.4'8994—dc22
2010004571

1 2 3 4 5 6 7 8 9 10 11 12 13 14 15 / 16 15 14 13 12 11 10

Rights for publishing this book outside the U.S.A. or in non-English languages are administered by Gospel Light Worldwide, an international not-for-profit ministry. For additional information, please visit www.glww.org, email info@glww.org, or write to Gospel Light Worldwide, 1957 Eastman Avenue, Ventura, CA 93003, U.S.A.

To order copies of this book and other Regal products in bulk quantities, please contact us at 1-800-446-7735.

Contents

Part IV: All Things Are Possible

Dedication and Acknowledgments

I dedicate this book to the growing number of believers in the Lord Jesus Christ worldwide who wish to grow in the supernatural life in a grounded manner, holding the cross of Jesus as the center of everything they do. I especially want to honor my dear late wife, Michal Ann Goll, who graduated to be with Jesus while I was preparing these materials. She lived the Christian life with an unusual mix of both the fruit and the gifts of the Spirit brought together in one vessel. I thank the Lord for the honor of living with this modern-day hero of the faith for more than 32 years. Heaven is fuller but earth is much emptier without her.

I am indebted to a number of key leaders who have had an impact on my life over the years, for whom I am very grateful. The list is long, so I will refrain from highlighting any specific individuals. I do wish to thank the Lord for Kathy Deering, my writing assistant, in this project. She is indeed one of the very best. I also wish to acknowledge the staff of Encounters Network, specifically my managing director, Jeffrey Thompson, and also Kim Bangs and team at Regal Books; I'm grateful to them for not giving up on me in the hour of my greatest trial.

I have composed this strategic book in hopes of seeing a new generation of true disciples of Jesus arise, men and women who walk in the double supernatural anointing of both character and power. With gratitude, I dedicate this book to be used as a tool arsenal for God's purposes in these last days.

With a love for God and His marvelous ways,

James W. Goll

This book is priceless in that it takes the supernatural lifestyle that has almost seemed out of reach and makes it accessible to every believer. To do this successfully, the author has to give hope and promise, and bathe these things in wisdom. James Goll has done this very well.

He is a rare prophet in that he is primarily a builder. Many similar ministries focus on tearing down so that another may come in and build. They have the assignment to expose things that are wrong. All prophets, including James, must do this in measure. But few are builders and architects of divine culture. James is.

James is a builder largely because he sees the heart of God for people and has had a glimpse of the outcome. As a result, his heart is filled with hope and promise; and out of that he continually pours out his life for the benefit of others. But he does so with amazing structure and excellence that only wisdom could conceive.

In part, *The Beginner's Guide to Signs, Wonders and the Supernatural Life* is a miracle in itself in that it was written in the midst of the greatest crisis of the author's life: the loss of his wife to cancer. Amazing to all who know him, James was able to live with extraordinary courage and faith, all while experiencing pain beyond description. While many would challenge God at this point concerning His goodness, or become embittered because of such horrible personal trials, James continued to pour out on these pages what has taken him decades of faithful service to learn: that God is always good, He is accessible, and that all believers can live like Jesus. As a result, we have a textbook on living in the supernatural, all the time.

I say "textbook" because of James's unusual ability to be foundational without sounding trite or simplistic. He has a gift for being thorough and the wisdom to be uniquely focused on the details that others would miss. We are the beneficiaries.

The apostle Paul had the assignment to write on the subject of "extreme joy" in his letter to Philippi. He wrote that epistle from prison—an oppressively dark, damp hole in the ground. I've seen it. And it's hard to imagine that something so joyful could come from that place. Such conflicts of soul can bring forth the richest truths, if the servant of the Lord restrains his or herself from the bitterness that consumes so many. While it would be improper to compare this book with Scripture, I do want to emphasize the process the Lord uses to bring forth ministry that is lasting. Much of what is done for the Lord in this day has a brief shelf life. But this book has the potential to leave its mark on many generations.

The Beginner's Guide to Signs, Wonders and the Supernatural Life comes to us at just the right time. It comes in response to the cries of a generation that wants to experience the authentic gospel that Jesus lived and taught. I pray that this book will end up in the right hands so that the generation that is willing to take a bullet for something will actually have a chance at the authentic lifestyle Jesus modeled for us all—living in the supernatural, naturally.

Bill Johnson
Senior Pastor, Bethel Church, Redding, California
Author of *When Heaven Invades Earth* and *Face to Face with God*

Part I
A Supernatural God

As believers in Jesus Christ, you and I walk in a supernatural life.

We don't have to search high and low for something called The Supernatural Life. It is already flowing through us. The reality of the new creation is this: When a person is born again, the Spirit of Jesus comes and takes up residence inside. From that moment forward, new life flows out of that person like a river of living water. As the *Amplified Bible* puts it: "He who believes in Me [who cleaves to and trusts in and relies on Me] as the Scripture has said, from his innermost being shall flow [continuously] springs and rivers of living water" (John 7:38).

The new life that flows through us makes it possible for the kingdom of God to touch the earth. "Jesus Christ is the same yesterday and today and forever" (Heb. 13:8). What He did from the beginning, He still does today—creating and re-creating, healing, restoring; sending light into the darkness; bringing victory to the humble and defeat to the proud. On a daily basis, we believers breathe the supernatural air of heaven.

Why, then, are most of us not aware of the supernatural aspect of our lives? Most of us seem to be dull to it. The difficulty must be more than just our all-too-human "feet of clay." We do not seem to know what we are missing.

Of course, many of us are quite aware of the invisible, supernatural life and its impact on our earthly lives, but we are a little afraid of it. We have seen people become overly fascinated with bizarre aspects of the "other side."

Where is the balance? Can we learn to distinguish between the good supernatural and the bad? How much awareness should we have of supernatural things? As followers of Jesus Christ, what should we be looking for?

Turn the page with me as we begin to explore what it means to be supernaturally natural—and naturally supernatural!

Chapter 1

Yesterday, Today and Forever

Any exploration of the supernatural life must begin on the firm foundation of Jesus Christ, because God has an enemy called Satan, and he is supernatural too. Satan is not as all-powerful as God, because he is an angel, one of God's created beings, who rebelled against his Creator and was banished from heaven to earth (see Luke 10:18; Isa. 14:12-17). But Satan is an enemy nonetheless, and he—along with the other supernatural beings who fell with him—seeks to undermine the reality of the life-bringing kingdom of God in the lives of believers.

One of Satan's favorite tactics is to confuse people about the supernatural life of the Kingdom. He wants people to forget that God is the same yesterday, today and forever. He wants people to remain ignorant of their access to the glories of Kingdom life. Furthermore, the enemy of God loves it when people think that "supernatural" refers to something that is spooky or evil, and that dabbling in anything that is supernatural is asking for trouble.

It is time to wake up! Unless we, as the sons and daughters of God, make a purposeful decision to live in the river of God's new life and learn about the Kingdom, we can be led astray into false loyalties and held captive to deceptive, dark spirits. We can be deprived of our birthright, which includes, while we are still on earth, multiple tastes of heaven and multiple encounters with the power of the living God, which are at the heart of a supernatural life.

Jesus Christ is the Light who overcomes the darkness (see John 9:5). He is the only firm foundation. When you walk in His light, you can experience—truly experience— the real, true, untainted supernatural glory and power of God. The apostle James wrote:

> Do not be deceived, my beloved brethren. Every good thing given and every perfect gift is from above, coming down from the Father of lights, with whom there is no variation or shifting shadow. In the exercise of His will He brought us forth by the word of truth, so that we would be a kind of first fruits among His creatures (Jas. 1:16-18, *NASB*).

Each time you treat someone with love, exercise a spiritual gift, surrender to the lordship of Jesus, seek guidance from God—not to mention each time you pray for (and receive) a miracle or achieve a victory over the power of darkness—you are living the supernatural life that Jesus won for you. Through you, the kingdom of God is making inroads into the kingdom of darkness.

We Live in a War Zone

Throughout the ages, the struggle between light and darkness has raged. Whether you like it or not, when you gave your life to Jesus, you were reborn into a war zone. The prizes of battle are individuals and even whole nations.

You cannot remain neutral in this war. If you remain neutral, by default you fall prey to the occupying forces of darkness. At the least, you will remain confused and disoriented, seeking counsel from wrong sources and building your life on a wobbly foundation. At the worst, you will sell out to the other side, turning away completely from God's love and wisdom, and trusting spiritual counterfeits. When you blur the lines between light and darkness, good and evil, you are left with a gray, hazy approach to discerning true spirituality—one that results in confusion and apathy on the one extreme or an inordinate hunger for supernatural power encounters on the other.

Living in the war zone is confusing. It is easy for people to call evil good and good evil. This happens not only in the world at large, but also within the walls of the Church. Then people consult psychics or buy into the latest pseudo-Christian philosophy. They take classes in how to read tarot cards or they watch paranormal demonstrations of people who "cross over" to visit dead relatives and bring back messages of comfort. Media celebrities lend their names to "spiritual" causes that lead their fans astray. In the name of inclusiveness, witches, warlocks and other neo-pagans are allowed to bring their occult practices into mainstream society.

As a result, the word "supernatural," which should mean simply "beyond the natural, observable, physical world," ends up tainted. It gets a black eye. The people who do not rush off to embrace everything labeled "supernatural" without discrimination tend to reject the gospel message (which is amazingly supernatural), considering it as much a figment of human imagination as the Easter Bunny.

Who Wins?

If you have read the end of the Book you know that God has already won this war. The decisive battle occurred on the hill of Calvary when, through the sacrifice of His Son, Jesus, God not only liberated human beings from demonic domination, but He also destroyed the very base of satanic rule. Satan's base had been established in the human race through pride, rebellion, disobedience, deceit, darkness and destruction. Now He had to contend with the King of Glory Himself, walking as a man in humble submission to His Father, in every point obedient, shining with light and exposing every lie, not destroying the world, but drawing it to Himself.

Jesus destroyed the rotten foundation that Satan had worked so hard to establish. He destroyed the works of the devil, which included sin and sickness, suffering and torment, rejection, shame, poverty and abandonment, and He exchanged them for eternal life. Now people would no longer have to wander like lost sheep. Their Shepherd had come to save them from their enemies. He had made them free to receive by faith all that belonged to the eternal Son of God.

When Jesus cried out from the cross, "It is finished" (John 19:30) and surrendered His Spirit, it was more than the completion of His life on earth. It was the complete destruction of the old regime. Darkness had lost.

Light had prevailed. The veil between heaven and earth was ripped in two. People could now enter heaven, following their Saving Shepherd, who had risen from the dead and was now seated securely at the right hand of His Father, constantly pleading their case as Advocate, waiting until all of the remaining rebels are brought into subjection as a result of the reverberation of His triumphal death and resurrection throughout the ages of the earth.[1]

People could now hear the words He spoke to His disciples when He sent them into the world as ambassadors of heaven, to proclaim and reveal His lordship:

> Jesus came up and spoke to them, saying, "All authority has been given to Me in heaven and on earth. Go therefore and make disciples of all the nations, baptizing them in the name of the Father and the Son and the Holy Spirit, teaching them to observe all that I commanded you; and lo, I am with you always, even to the end of the age" (Matt. 28:18-20, *NASB*).

Because of the Cross

The work of the cross of Christ made it possible for believers in Him to receive right standing with the Father. Jesus' righteousness became theirs. They could now enter into fellowship and favor with God. Satan had been deprived of his one great weapon. The people who put their trust in Jesus could be forgiven for their rebellion against God (see John 1:12).

In one master stroke, God accomplished three things:

1. He defeated Satan (see Heb. 2:14).
2. He took away Satan's legal authority to rule over the human race.
3. He restored the blessings that Satan had stolen from the human race.

Satan, however, was and is still alive and kicking. Having always been a thief, a deceiver and the father of lies, he never has and never will play "fair." He will never play by the rules unless we, the people of God who live in the earth, enforce the victory of the cross.

Satan will unceasingly strive to keep God's people, also known as the Body of Christ, in a state of ignorance, darkness, weakness, disability and division. Satan knows something that most of us fail to recognize—that it is *through us* that God will punish him.

Through ordinary human beings like you and me, people who become naturally supernatural when they receive new life, Satan's darkness will be exposed to the light. He loses ground every day that the kingdom of God advances through the body of believers on the earth.

Inasmuch as it was Jesus' job to expose and destroy the works of the devil (see 1 John 3:8), that same job is now ours as His representatives in the world. Through believers, individually and collectively, His Spirit continues to expose the darkness by turning on the light of the completed work of the cross. By faith, we enforce the victory that Jesus Christ has already won.

Even if in our short lifetime we do not see every enemy fully under Jesus' feet, we do not give up. We learn from every setback and we continue to grow and to flow with new life. Here we are, ordinary men and women, walking around with a supernatural God living inside us. You and I live and breathe and have our being in Him (see Acts 17:28). The more intentional our walk in the power of the One who set us free, the more naturally supernatural we will be.

Boasting in the Cross

The cross of Jesus Christ is the intersection of the natural life and the supernatural life.

If I am going to boast in something, I want to boast in the significance and power of the cross. Jesus' cross is central to our salvation. Without it, the entire human race would be stumbling in darkness, hopeless and helpless. Because of the cross, the Light can shine.

The crucifixion of Jesus—the death and burial and subsequent resurrection of the Son of God—is a physical, historical fact (see Matt. 27; Mark 15; Luke 23; John 19). Even if you strip it of its supernatural aspects, it remains an actual series of events that took place in the city of Jerusalem more than 2,000 years ago. Jesus' friends and followers wrote careful accounts of what happened:

A man named Jesus of Nazareth was arrested by the authorities. It did not take long for the hastily convened court to convict and sentence Him to death on a cross, which was the Roman method for torturing and executing criminals. A few hours after being nailed to long pieces of wood alongside two lawbreakers, He died. Grieving, a handful of His friends retrieved His bloody remains and buried Him in a borrowed tomb. Three days later, by which time the rest of the city had resumed its normal affairs, His tomb was found empty. As the days turned into weeks, He Himself was spotted several times, and He spoke with those who had known Him before He was killed.

This really happened. It is not good fiction. It is not a fairy tale. It is an accurate, historical account.

Eventually, He stopped appearing to them, leaving each one of His friends and followers (and all those who would later believe, including us) with a deposit of His Holy Spirit in their hearts. In hindsight, Jesus' followers could now see the significance of the cross. They could see how the natural, historical events had been penetrated by the intentional acts of a supernatural God. An exchange had been made.

Jesus' followers could see how the cross had become the intersection of heaven and earth. The supernatural traffic between heaven and earth could flow freely through this intersection, and every individual who assented to Jesus—not just the super-special priests and prophets—could experience supernatural life.

Exchanging Punishment for Peace

Seven centuries before Jesus' crucifixion, the prophet Isaiah wrote down an amazing messianic prophecy. Here is one line from it: "He was wounded for our transgressions, He was bruised for our iniquities; the chastisement for our peace was upon Him" (Isa. 53:5, *NKJV*).

On the cross, Jesus received, in His body and soul, the punishment that was due to each sinful human being. Because He—One who was sinless and who in no way deserved it—submitted to it, He paid the penalty for anyone who believes in what He did. With the penalty paid, you and I do not have to pay it ourselves. We would be relegated to eternal punishment if we did.

With the penalty paid, the exchange can be made. Peace, reconciliation and forgiveness can replace chaos, banishment and shame. That is good news!

Exchanging Sickness for Healing

Isaiah spoke of another exchange: "He has borne our griefs and carried our sorrows . . . by His stripes we are healed" (Isa. 53:4-5, *NKJV*). Matthew quoted this passage directly (see Matt. 8:17) and so did his fellow apostle Peter (see 1 Pet. 2:24). When Jesus was whipped and beaten and then crucified, He bore in His own body our pain and sickness, transforming them from being the natural outcome of our human condition to elements ready for supernatural healing and restoration.

So already we have two significant exchanges: (1) a spiritual one—punishment exchanged for peace, and (2) a physical one—sickness exchanged for healing.

Exchanging Sin for Righteousness

Paul's statement in his second letter to the Corinthians reflects other biblical statements. Explaining the significance of the cross, Paul wrote, "God made him who had no sin to be sin for us, so that in him we might become the righteousness of God" (2 Cor. 5:21).

This was foreshadowed by Moses, when the people of Israel were being bitten and killed by venomous snakes, and God told Moses to make a bronze snake and put it high up on a pole so that the people could look at it and exchange the punishment of death for safety from death (see Num. 21:4-9). Tying these events together in his Gospel, John wrote, "As Moses lifted up the serpent in the wilderness, even so must the Son of Man be lifted up; so that whoever believes in Him will have eternal life" (John 3:14-15, *NASB*).

Later, John also made it clear that this exchange applied both to sinful nature and the sinful acts that it produces (see 1 John 1:8-10). The amazing thing about the cross is that Jesus did not die only so that our sins (plural) could be forgiven. He came to deliver the deathblow to our old sin nature itself, making it possible for us to receive His righteousness.

On the cross, Jesus was made sick with our sicknesses in order that we might be made whole with His health. It was the Father's will to allow His Son to be "bruised unto sickness" (see Isa. 53:10) and smitten and sick (see Mic. 6:13). Our holy God set it up so that He could reconcile the rebellious, sinful human race to Himself. As Isaiah put it: "Thou shalt make his soul an offering for sin" (Isa. 53:10, *KJV*).

Exchanging Curse for Blessing

On the cross, Jesus was cursed with the curse of our sinfulness so that we might be blessed with the wholeness of spiritual, physical, mental and emotional provision. The picture of the body of Jesus on the cross is a picture of His identification with our rebellion and its consequences. The picture of His resurrected body shows us what He has won for us. Anyone who puts his or her faith in the name of Jesus can exchange the curse they started out with for the Father's complete endorsement and blessing.

Many Christians are enduring a curse when they should be enjoying a blessing. They are struggling with unfruitfulness, insufficiency, frustration, failure, defeat, bondage, poverty, fear, physical and mental illness and more (see Deut. 28:15-68). If you are a New Testament believer who is "seated with Christ Jesus in heavenly places" (see Eph. 1:20), you can expect to enjoy the blessings of fruitfulness, abundance, protection, direction, victory, success, holiness, honor and dominion (see Deut. 28:1-14).

It is true that we have come under a curse because of our inability to observe the whole law continually (see Gal. 3:10). But Jesus Christ took upon Himself the curse that was due to us for breaking God's law, so that we might receive the blessings that are due to Christ's obedience.

With our own strength, none of us can walk in perfection; but thanks to being able to walk in Jesus' perfect obedience, the blessings replace the curses. "He leads me in the paths of righteousness for His name's sake. . . . Surely goodness and mercy shall follow me all the days of my life" (Ps. 23:3,6, *NKJV*).

Faith in Jesus provides perfect soundness (see Acts 3:16), and it makes the exchange complete between punishment and reward (see Isa. 52:13-15; 3 John 2).

Exchanging Poverty for Wealth

Paul spoke of the magnificent exchange that Jesus offers us: "For you know the grace of our Lord Jesus Christ, that though he was rich, yet for your sakes he became poor, so that you through his poverty might become rich" (2 Cor. 8:9). The grace through which this exchange is accomplished has only one channel, and that is Jesus Himself, because of His cross.

It is God's will for us to serve Him with joyfulness and gladness for the abundance and provision that He brings our way (see Deut. 28:47). Instead, many of us settle for the alternative, which is to serve our enemies in hunger, thirst, nakedness and poverty (see Deut. 28:48).

However, thanks to the favorable "exchange rate" of the cross, God is able to flood us with His grace in abundance: "And God is able to make all grace abound toward you, that you, always having all sufficiency in all things, may have an abundance for every good work" (2 Cor. 9:8, *NKJV*).

Provision instead of destitution. Abundance in exchange for lack. Wealth in place of poverty. This is just the "main and the plain" of what Jesus has done on the cross.

Exchanging Threefold Death for Threefold Life

Jesus died on the cross "that He, by the grace of God, might taste death for everyone" (Heb. 2:9). He tasted death in three successive phases: (1) He was cut off from union and fellowship with the Father; (2) He was cut off from physical life; and (3) He was banished from God's presence like a scapegoat, carrying sin away.[2]

Jesus had never known one second of uncontaminated communion with the Father until He was nailed to that cross. Suddenly, He could no longer see or hear or sense His Father's presence. Because the Father cannot look upon sin, He closed His eyes to His Son, who was being obliterated by the accumulated sins of the human race.

Jesus was cut off so that we might be grafted in. He was crucified and buried; He descended into Hades and rose again so that our redemption could be complete. The exchange could be made. In exchange, the gift of life to every believer is also a threefold one: (1) union and fellowship with God; (2) physical resurrection life in our mortal bodies; and (3) resurrection and eternal life in God's glorious presence.[3]

Exchanging the Old Man for the New

With Jesus on the cross, our old human nature was executed. After it was dead and gone, it was resurrected to new, supernatural life. Do you want to know who your "new man" is? It is Christ Jesus who lives in you by means of your faith.

Your old nature, which you inherited from your ancestor Adam, and which is inherently sinful, has been replaced (see Rom. 6:6; 8:10; Col. 2:11; Gal. 5:17-24). From the moment you said yes to Jesus, you have been flowing with the life of Jesus. You have exchanged your former bondage for freedom. Now you have Kingdom options. Now you have grace. Now you have strength. Now you have wisdom. Now you have an obedient mind and a willing heart.

What an exchange!

The Cross Means the Devil's Defeat

Because of the cross of Jesus Christ, you and I can live a supernatural life. We can live a supernatural life because the devil, under whom we formerly lived, has been cast off (see John 12:31). We can live the supernatural life because we have a new foundation; we have exchanged our rotten, sin-saturated foundation for the firm foundation of Jesus' righteousness.

The work of Jesus Christ on the cross has made it possible for all members of the human race to receive His righteousness and enter into fellowship and favor with God. Those who accept this have deprived Satan of his great weapon against God and man. Satan has been stripped and humiliated. Jesus has "disarmed the powers and authorities, he made a public spectacle of them, triumphing over them by the cross" (Col. 2:15).

Satan's great weapon has always been accusation. Before the cross, he had had actual grounds for accusation. Now he is reduced to pretense and posturing. If enough people will believe him enough of the time, he can continue to make a good showing. But nothing he can do can undo his defeat. He can only try to interfere as God actively restores the blessings of which Satan had robbed humankind. He and his evil cohorts can only strive to keep people in a state of condemnation, ignorant of their standing as sons and daughters of the living God.

Walking in the Privilege of New Life

Because the cross means the Devil's defeat, it means victory for all who name the name of Jesus. Sharing in the victory that He won through His death on the cross and His resurrection, we share in the glorious privileges and blessings of eternal, supernatural life.

It is our honor to be ambassadors of Christ in the world. It is our joy to let His light shine through our lives. It is our privilege to manifest the signs of the kingdom of God wherever we go. Jesus said, "These signs will accompany those who believe: In my name they will drive out demons; they will speak in new tongues; they will pick up snakes with their hands; and when they drink deadly poison, it will not hurt them at all; they will place their hands on sick people, and they will get well" (Matt. 16:17-18).

Those signs are supernatural. They are part of your birthright. The supernatural God who never changes has restored them to you. Hold out your hands to receive all that He wants to give you as a born-again, Spirit-filled follower of Jesus Christ.

Review

Because those who have put their faith in Jesus Christ have become citizens of the kingdom of heaven, it is part of the birthright of every Christian to live a supernatural life.

1. Have you carried concern about mistakenly becoming involved with the kingdom of darkness? How can you make sure that you don't?

2. What three things did Jesus accomplish on the cross?

3. The cross is the place where the natural life and the supernatural life intersect. On the cross, a significant exchange was made. List eight aspects of that exchange.

Chapter 2

The Dynamic Holy Spirit

One important principle of Bible interpretation is the "law of first mention," which means that you need to pay particular attention to the first time something is mentioned in Scripture, because subsequent "mentions" will need to be interpreted in light of that first time.

Where is the Holy Spirit first mentioned in the Bible? Right away, in the second verse of the very first chapter, in a line that is so familiar to us: "The earth was formless and void, and darkness was over the surface of the deep, and the Spirit of God was moving over the surface of the waters" (Gen. 1:2, *NASB*).

That very first time He is mentioned in Scripture, what was the Holy Spirit of God doing? *Moving.* He was in motion; He was energetic; He was dynamic. One dictionary entry defines "dynamic" this way: "marked by usually continuous and productive activity or change."

The verse does not indicate that this moving was stopped after the Creation was completed or that it was a historical, special, one-time moving. No, the Holy Spirit—who, you will remember, is the same yesterday, today and forever—was continuously moving then, and He is continuously moving now. Later in the Bible, He is compared to the wind, invisible to our eyes but always in motion from one place to another (see John 3:8).

Sadly, this is not the way that most of the Church thinks of the Holy Spirit. Reinforced by the Apostles' Creed, churchgoers lose sight of the Holy Spirit, or Holy Ghost, because He is mentioned so briefly. In the Creed, we repeat many details about the Father and the Son. Yet about the Holy Spirit, we recite only six words: "I believe in the Holy Ghost." That's it. No wonder we lose sight of the Holy Spirit.

God, we may claim to know. Jesus, we may say we love. But the third Person of the godhead, the Holy Spirit? We are a little vague about Him. We forget that He is a person; we call Him an "it." We don't pray to Him. We forget to give Him credit for what He does. He is a "ghost"? You mean, He's like the cartoon character Casper, the Friendly Ghost? We don't quite get it.

Of course, "ghost" is just another word for "spirit," and it was in common usage when the *King James Version* of the Bible was written. The word "spirit" provides us with an important link to our own experience of His dynamic, supernatural presence in our lives, because it is through our own human spirits that we will always encounter Him. Living the supernatural life involves communication between our spirits and His Spirit, and His Spirit to ours.

How to Relate to Him

As He moves through our lives and over our spirits, He creates order out of chaos, just as He did at the beginning of time. That's His job. He loves to move in the midst of darkness, and that is where He is needed most.

We can participate with His dynamic motion, spirit to Spirit, or we can move away from Him, retreating back into the darkness we came from. We have a choice in the matter.

I am assuming that you are reading this book in order to move toward Him and with Him. Let's consider various ways to relate to Him, some positive and some negative.

Positive Responses to the Holy Spirit

To live a supernatural life, you need to become friends with the Holy Spirit. By that, I do not mean that you become overly familiar with Him, too "chummy," offhand and casual. You need to honor Him, always. He is God. Yet He wishes to relate with you, and you can respond to His desire.

Seek Him. Look for Him. Ask for Him. Seek to be equipped by Him. He wants to visit you and He wants to be your equipper. Ask the Father in Jesus' name to equip you by the Holy Spirit to do the ministry work to which He has called you. Greet Him daily.

Honor Him as a guest. Welcome Him on a first-name basis, acknowledging Him as the third Person of the Godhead, the one Person of the Godhead who is resident in the earth today. He has come to you, so welcome Him and give Him the best seat in the house. With His own distinct personality, He has come to guide you (see John 16:13).

Jesus said that He would have to leave, but that the Father would send us another Helper, a Paraclete, a Holy Spirit, One called alongside to help (see John 14:16,26; 15:26; 16:7). Welcome Him because you desire His presence. Be glad that He has come.

Give Him freedom and liberty. Let the Holy Spirit be in control of your life. If you say you want to live the supernatural life, then give the Spirit free rein.

If you give Him the freedom to control your life, you will be free from everything else that has ever taken control of you. "Now the Lord is the Spirit, and where the Spirit of the Lord is, there is freedom" (2 Cor. 3:17). Conversely, if you do *not* give Him freedom and liberty in your life, you will not be able to find true freedom, no matter how hard you try.

By the way, many believers like to say that they are "open to the Holy Spirit," but I cannot find that phrase anywhere in the Bible. As far as I can tell, God does not want us to be merely "open" to Him. People may think they are doing God a great favor by being open to His Spirit, but that is only the very first step. By itself, it is an incomplete step.

You need to take action, with passion. You need to pursue Him. You need to earnestly desire spiritual gifts and stir them up (see 1 Cor. 12:31; 14:1; 2 Tim. 1:6).

Be born of the Spirit. When Nicodemus came to talk to Jesus, he did not understand how to be "born again," so Jesus explained:

> In reply Jesus declared, "I tell you the truth, no one can see the kingdom of God unless he is born again."
>
> "How can a man be born when he is old?" Nicodemus asked. "Surely he cannot enter a second time into his mother's womb to be born!"
>
> Jesus answered, "I tell you the truth, no one can enter the kingdom of God unless he is born of

water and the Spirit. Flesh gives birth to flesh, but the Spirit gives birth to spirit. You should not be surprised at my saying, 'You must be born again.' The wind blows wherever it pleases. You hear its sound, but you cannot tell where it comes from or where it is going. So it is with everyone born of the Spirit" (John 3:3-8).

The foremost positive response to the Spirit of God is to allow Him to bring you to new life. Be born of the Spirit. I am a Spirit man. You are a Spirit man or a Spirit woman. We are born from above, from the Spirit of the Living God.

Receive and be baptized in the Spirit. When you got baptized in water, you got wet. You got saturated with the water. When you get baptized in the Holy Spirit, you get saturated with the Spirit.

The prophet John the Baptist said, "I baptize you with water for repentance. But after me will come one who is more powerful than I, whose sandals I am not fit to carry. He will baptize you with the Holy Spirit and with fire" (Matt. 3:11). He was referring to his cousin Jesus, whom he would soon baptize in water, but whom he recognized as the One who would baptize with the Spirit.

When Jesus was on the verge of leaving His disciples, He told them to wait for the promised Holy Spirit, who would empower them to carry on the signs and the work of His kingdom. He told them, "you will receive power when the Holy Spirit has come upon you; and you shall be my witnesses both in Jerusalem, and in all Judea and Samaria, and even to the remotest part of the earth" (Acts 1:8).

Don't even try to do the work of the Spirit without the Holy Spirit! Receive Him.

Be continuously filled. Receiving the Holy Spirit is not a one-time thing. It is not something you do only on Christmas or Easter or Pentecost. It is an ongoing thing. You and I need to be filled continuously with God's Spirit. Why? Because we leak! (Very simple theology.) Because we dispense God's glory wherever we go, and we need to be refilled, and the refilling needs to be a continuous process.

In his letter to the Ephesian church, Paul wrote, "Do not get drunk with wine, for that is debauchery; but ever be filled and stimulated with the [Holy] Spirit" (Eph. 5:18, *AMP*). The *Amplified Version* captures the sense of the original Greek verb, which indicates the idea of continual filling and refilling.

Know and see the Spirit. The world at large cannot know and see the Spirit, but you can, because He lives with you and in you. Jesus explained it this way:

> I will ask the Father, and he will give you another Counselor to be with you forever—the Spirit of truth. The world cannot accept him, because it neither sees him nor knows him. But you know him, for he lives with you and will be in you. I will not leave you as orphans; I will come to you (John 14:16-18).

Jesus has asked the Father to send us the Holy Spirit so that we will not have to wander around blind and clueless. Because of the Spirit inside us, we really can know God. We really can be "seers," in the truest sense of the word. This is one of the things we are supposed to do as born-again believers. We really can know Him. We can experience Him. He mirrors the Son. He acts like the Father. He counsels us and points us to the truth.

Be led by the Spirit. In order to be "led," you have to have a leader. A leader does not drive you like a mule or an ox or a slave driver. A leader leads, and you follow. This is very basic.

Romans 8:14 tells us that "those who are led by the Spirit of God are sons of God." Those who are sons and daughters of the King are secure in their identity. They don't have to perform to earn their position. Freely they can follow the wishes of the King—without undue pressure. After all, He is in the lead, just as in a dance. All you have to do is allow yourself to be led by Him.

Being led by the Spirit of God is different from being led by religion. If you allow yourself to be led by religion, you are going to be driven by rules and laws. You will be influenced by a political spirit. You will become more and more bound up instead of free.

Pray in the Spirit. In response to the Holy Spirit, you must say something. You must pray, converse with Him; you pray in the Spirit: "You, dear friends, build yourselves up in your most holy faith and pray in the Holy Spirit" (Jude 1:20).

One of the best ways to pray in the Spirit is to pray in tongues. We need to rediscover this gift. When you pray in the Spirit, you can move out from under the limits of your own rational understanding. "Trust in the Lord with all your heart and lean not on your own understanding" (Prov. 3:5). The proverb goes on to say, "In all your ways acknowledge Him, and He shall direct your paths" (Prov. 3:6, *NKJV*).

Respond to Him, acknowledge Him, pray in Him, and He will lead you to exactly the right place in exactly the right way.

Hear the Spirit. The writer of the letter to the Hebrews quotes a psalm when he encourages them to listen to the Spirit—and to respond with willing obedience (see Heb. 3:15). He is quoting from Psalm 95 (emphasis added):

> Come, let us bow down in worship,
> > let us kneel before the Lord our Maker;
> for he is our God
> > and we are the people of his pasture,
> > > the flock under his care.
> > *Today, if you hear his voice,*
> *do not harden your hearts* as you did at Meribah,
> > as you did that day at Massah in the desert,
> where your fathers tested and tried me,
> > though they had seen what I did (Ps. 95:6-9).

You will not always hear Him, but you should always listen for Him. You won't want to miss His voice.

Walk in the Spirit. "Walking in the Spirit" is the same as living a supernatural, Spirit-saturated, Spirit-led life. When you walk according to the moment-by-moment guidance of the Spirit, you will sidestep sin: "Live by the Spirit, and you will not gratify the desires of the sinful nature" (Gal. 5:13).

Walking in the Spirit incorporates all of the positive responses to the Holy Spirit: seeking Him and honoring

Him; giving Him free rein; being baptized and continuously filled with Him; knowing, seeing, hearing and being led by Him; and conversing with Him in prayer.

My favorite definition of moving in the Holy Spirit is this: flowing with the Lord so as to not cast two shadows. That's living and walking in the Holy Spirit.

Negative Responses to the Holy Spirit

In the Bible, we see the Holy Spirit coming upon Jesus in the form of a dove (see Matt. 3:16). John the Baptist testified that he saw the dove descend and remain (see John 1:32).

Now, a dove is notorious for being shy. Doves do not remain anyplace where they feel threatened. As much as we may want Him to descend and remain, and as many "descending meetings" we attend, we cannot expect Him to remain for long if we fail to prepare a welcoming environment for Him. If He descends, I want Him to stay. I want to be a perch! I want to be like Jesus, one onto whom He descends and with whom He remains.

Here are a few common "scare tactics" that we should try to avoid if we desire to host the Holy Spirit dove.

Do not be ignorant. Do not neglect the abundant resources you have been given. Study to show yourself approved to God, one of His own (see 2 Tim. 2:15). Have you studied about the Holy Spirit? Have you studied the nature of the Holy Spirit? Have you studied about the fruit of the Spirit and the gifts of the Spirit? Have you learned about the ministries of the Spirit?

Paul uses the word "ignorant" 13 times in his epistles, expressing his disapproval of ignorant believers. For example, in his letter to the Corinthians, he writes, "Now about spiritual gifts, brothers, I do not want you to be ignorant" (1 Cor. 12:1). Avoid ignorance by becoming a lifelong learner. Be like Mary of Bethany. Sit at His feet and soak up all that you can.

Do not grieve the Spirit. We are very familiar with the following passage of Scripture, but do we take it personally and seriously?

> Do not let any unwholesome talk come out of your mouths, but only what is helpful for build-ing others up according to their needs, that it may benefit those who listen. And *do not grieve the Holy Spirit of God,* with whom you were sealed for the day of redemption. Get rid of all bitterness, rage and anger, brawling and slander, along with every form of malice (Eph. 4:29-31, emphasis added).

Do you sometimes speak angry words? Have you har-bored malice or bitterness? Have you uttered words that tear down your listeners, filling them with shame or fear? Have you murmured or complained? Have you expressed unbelief? One of the primary ways we can grieve the Spirit is through our mouths—our speech.

You can turn it around. I know; this is one of my per-sonal struggles. I don't want the Holy Spirit dove to be a mourning dove, and neither do you. I want to be thank-ful and praiseful. I want to be forgiving and grace giving. I want to speak good things about others, never slander-ing them or accusing them. I want to attract the Holy Spirit by maintaining (with His help) a pure heart and wholesome, life-giving speech.

Do not quench the Spirit. First Thessalonians 5:19 is another familiar passage: "Do not quench the Spirit" (*NASB, NKJV*). The *New International Version* translates it this way: "Do not put out the Spirit's fire." My Goll-amplified paraphrased version is: "Don't be a wet blanket."

Instead, rejoice with those who rejoice (see Rom. 12:15). Be complementary to the Holy Spirit, not a contradiction to Him. Let His light shine out through you. Don't snuff it or quench it.

Do not blaspheme against the Spirit. That is certainly a strong one. In fact, it has given rise to much needless anxiety about committing the "unforgivable sin." The prohibition appears in three of the Gospels: in Matthew 12:31-32, Mark 3:28-29, and Luke 12:10. In every case, Jesus is being quoted as saying that He would forgive those who speak against Him or the Father, but that cursing the Holy Spirit is a different matter.

The word "blaspheme" literally means "to curse" or to speak evil of someone. People use the name of Jesus and God in vain all day long. It's not good, but it's forgivable. But once you have repudiated the name of the Spirit, you have blocked out all that God is. You have fallen into unbelief. You have repudiated the very source of your life.

When the Pharisees accused Jesus of doing His works by the power of a demon named "Beelzebub," they were blaspheming against the Spirit (see Matt. 12:24). The blasphemy was attributing Jesus' power to the devil rather than to the Holy Spirit. Jesus made this clear when He said, " 'But whoever blasphemes against the Holy Spirit will never be forgiven; he is guilty of an eternal sin.' He

said this because they were saying, 'He has an evil spirit'"
(Mark 3:29-30).

Bottom line: Don't speak against the Holy Spirit, making Him out to be evil. Don't even get close to doing it.

Do not insult the Holy Spirit. When you insult someone, what do they do? They remove themselves from your presence. When you have been insulted, what do you do? You get out of that place as fast as you can. If you have to stay, at the least you disengage; you close your heart off; you back off.

The Bible compares insults of other human beings or human institutions to insulting the Spirit: How much more severely do you think a man deserves to be punished who has trampled the Son of God underfoot, who has treated as an unholy thing the blood of the covenant that sanctified him, and who has insulted the Spirit of grace (see Heb. 10:29)?

People can insult the Spirit by treating Him like a genie in a bottle, by bargaining with Him, belittling Him in the process. You can insult the Spirit when you put yourself above Him as a judge, "explaining Him away" by giving some other reason for one of His manifestations. In the heat of the moment, it can be easy to do. But if you insult the Holy Spirit, don't be surprised if He backs off.

Do not tempt or test the Holy Spirit. Events in the New Testament Church provide us with a horrifyingly vivid example, in the life and death of Ananias and Sapphira, of what it means to tempt the Holy Spirit. This married couple wanted to appear to be as generous as other believers when it came to giving donations to the church.

So they sold some property in order to donate the proceeds. But then they conspired together to withhold some of the money for themselves, while lying about it.

It's not a good idea to try to deceive the Holy Spirit! Never test His tolerance for that sort of thing. Peter discerned the plot. First, Ananias was struck dead; and a little later, so was Sapphira. When she affirmed the lie, Peter said to her, "How could you agree to test the Spirit of the Lord? Look! The feet of the men who buried your husband are at the door, and they will carry you out also" (Acts 5:9).

While subsequent instances of lying to the Holy Spirit may not have been punished quite as severely, nevertheless it is never a good idea to lie to the Holy Spirit. He knows everything. He *knows*. And He will not bless it.

Throw away comparisons. In a slightly different vein, another way to discourage the Holy Spirit's presence in your life is to contrast and compare yourself to other people, for better or for worse. You are not meant to conform to their image or to their ideal; you are meant to conform to Him, and His way of expressing Himself through you will be distinctive and unique.

When you have your eyes on the other person, you take your eyes off of Him. So if you want to preserve your ability to respond to the Holy Spirit, don't remain ignorant of what He is like. Respect His opinion most of all, even if it comes at your expense. Fill your heart and mind with godly thoughts and motives. Repent as fast as possible when your conscience (informed by the Spirit) tugs at your awareness.

How Does the Spirit Move?

Before He left them, Jesus explained to His disciples that the Holy Spirit would come and dwell in them, and that He would show them how to proceed on a daily basis (see John 14:16-21 and John 16:5-15). Although it is true that the Spirit wants to lead us, and it is true that He is like the wind, a lot of people have taken this to mean that all you need to do to move with Him is to set your sails, catch the wind and go. They pay no attention to the principles of sailing.

1. *I will not teach someone to set sail without an anchor.* I will not give someone a kite to fly without a spindle to hold on to. I will not tell you to move with the Spirit without giving you some idea of the most typical ways He moves.

2. *The Spirit moves through the written Word.* He never moves contrary to the Scriptures. He complements the written Word; He does not compete with it.

3. *The Spirit moves in agreement with the Father and the Son.* The Godhead never experiences or expresses conflict, but rather, one unified will. The Holy Spirit reveals the counsel of the Father and the Son.

4. *The Spirit brings Jesus into better focus.* He reveals Jesus in all of His living reality, and He brings us into a deeper relationship with our Savior.

5. *The Spirit connects us with the source of life.* He is more interested in maturing your character than in bringing you personal comfort. He will bring you truth rather than false assurance or consolation. He will woo, convict, shepherd and lead you to God the Father and Jesus His Son, who are your life-source.

6. *The Spirit moves believers to become witnesses.* He will help you overcome your fears and He will stretch you outside of yourself, bringing both maturity and fruit. He will motivate you to testify of the love and power of God.

If you stop and think about it, you will realize that the Holy Spirit is the first person of the Godhead that you actually met. He is the one who stood at the door of your heart and knocked until you opened the door to God (see Rev. 3:20). He revealed your need for God, and He made Jesus real to you. He is moving in the same way in your life today.

How Can You Flow in the Holy Spirit?

This book is *The Beginner's Guide to Signs, Wonders and the Supernatural Life*. It could have been called *The Beginner's Guide to Flowing in the Holy Spirit*, because living the supernatural life is all about flowing in the Spirit.

How can you best prepare yourself to "go with the flow" of the Spirit? I have already mentioned one very important way: pray in the Spirit, using the gift of tongues. When you pray in the Spirit, you "build yourself up" in your faith (see Jude 1:20). You practice His presence. You sing in the Spirit and you worship from your heart. Your heart widens. Your ability to communicate with Him increases. So one of the primary ways you can increase the flow of the Holy Spirit is to pray in the Spirit.

In preparation to flow in the Holy Spirit, anytime, anyplace, you need to quiet your own spirit. Avoid hurrying. Stop rushing. Quiet yourself before the Lord. Do not let your spirit and soul be like a stirred-up fish bowl or a shaken-up snow globe. Just rest in His presence:

> I have stilled and quieted my soul;
>> like a weaned child with its mother,
>> like a weaned child is my soul within me
> (Ps. 131:2).

> I wait for the Lord, my soul waits,
>> And in His word I do hope.
> My soul waits for the Lord
>> More than those who watch for the morning—
>> Yes, more than those who watch for the morning (Ps. 130:5-6, NKJV).

Quiet yourself so that you can receive from Him. Receiving from Him is an intentional act. You have to get involved. You cannot be passive, or nothing will happen.

Seek God for something to take with you when you attend a gathering of believers. Decide in your heart that you want to give more than you want to receive. Yes, God will use little ol' you! His Spirit will flow through you to impart something to others. God wants to use your heart, your hands, your tears, your laughter, your sorrow—your whole being—to make a connection between Him and the people around you. He can use you anyplace; you don't have to be in church. Seek Him for something to take when you are going to the shopping mall—seriously. Flow in His Spirit wherever you go.

As you go, ask Him for a revelation of His grace. That way all the glory will go to Him, and not to you. Your testimony will not belong to you; it will belong to Him. It will be the testimony of Jesus Christ in the present tense, the ministry of the Holy Spirit today, not the testimony of you or your spouse or James Goll or Billy Graham. If it is a valid testimony of the Spirit, it belongs to Him. And it will make a difference of some sort. It will leave an impression.

Your contribution will be distinctive, because you are distinctive. God created you with a specific, personalized mixture of gifts and talents. But if you are flowing with the Holy Spirit, the supernatural life will always be His: "There are diversities of gifts, but the same Spirit. There are differences of ministries, but the same Lord. And there are diversities of activities, but it is the same God who works all in all" (1 Cor. 12:4-6, *NKJV*).

The creative life of the Spirit broods over His own people, energizing them in special ways, more diverse and numerous than we can comprehend, bringing heavenly light to earthly darkness. From the beginning, the Spirit has desired to find those through whom He could manifest Himself.

In the Creation, He "hovered" like a brooding hen over her baby chicks (see Gen. 1:2). In the wilderness with Moses, two otherwise nameless Israelites started prophesying (see

Num. 11:26-30). Moses' response is timeless: "Would that all the Lord's people were prophets, that the Lord would put His Spirit upon them!" (Num. 11:29, *NASB*).

The prophet Joel foretold a day when prophecy, dreams and visions would become widespread (see Joel 2:28-29). After Jesus came, and after He bestowed His Spirit on the people who had believed everything that He had told them, the apostle Peter exclaimed that the day Joel had prophesied had arrived (see Acts 2:14-21).

You and I are living in that day. God is ministering the supernatural gifts of the Holy Spirit to those who hunger for Him and honor Him. Give Him free rein. Ask for more of His Spirit. May He hover over you and bring His order out of your life, making it a supernatural, God-infused life.

Review

The Holy Spirit is the sole key to the supernatural life. How you relate to the Spirit will determine how "supernatural" your life will become.

1. Why do we say the Holy Spirit is "dynamic"?

2. List and discuss three positive responses you have made to the Holy Spirit. Have you ever fallen into one of the negative responses to Him? What did you do about it?

3. From the suggestions in this chapter, name two of your favorite ways to make the Holy Spirit welcome in your life.

Chapter 3

Filled and Overflowing

When I was in high school, I loved science, especially biology. One thing I learned is that you dissect something only after it is dead.

That may be one of the problems with any in-depth discussion of the Holy Spirit. The Holy Spirit is far from dead, and yet we attempt to examine and analyze Him almost as if He were a lab specimen.

The other problem is that the Holy Spirit is *God*. So isn't it a bit presumptuous for us to assume that we can figure Him out? Yet studying the evidence and putting it all together is the only way we can take the next steps into living our new life in a way that is fully supernatural. We need to know how to become fully immersed in the Holy Spirit. With childlike openness and responsiveness, let us resume our exploration of the third Person of the Trinity.

He Came, and He Stayed

In the midst of the disciples' fear and uncertainty after Jesus' death, the resurrected Jesus comforted them about His imminent ascension to heaven by promising them that He would send another one to be with them on earth. He told them that they would receive another Helper or Comforter. The Greek word is *parakletos,* from which we derive our English word "paraclete," which means one who is summoned to someone's side to assist and to give aid, even to be a legal assistant or an advocate before a judge (see John 14:12-18,25-26; 15:26; 16:5-15).

His promise was to the disciples, and it is for us to this day. As Jesus promised, the Paraclete will do all of the following:

- He will be with us forever to comfort and strengthen us.
- He will dwell in us.
- He will teach us all things.
- He will bring to our remembrance the words of Jesus.
- He will bear witness to Jesus.
- He will convict the world of sin.
- He will guide us into all truth.
- He will glorify Jesus.
- He will give us power.

He will do all of these things because of His nature. He is always making the connection between Himself and believers, in whose heart He dwells.

Names for the Spirit in Scripture

The Holy Spirit is known by many names in the Bible, and each one of them portrays a particular aspect of His nature. Among many descriptive names, He is known as:

- *Spirit of the Lord, of Wisdom, of Understanding, of Counsel, of Might, of Knowledge, and of Fear of the*

Lord (often called the seven-fold Spirit of God; see Isa. 11:1-3)
• *Spirit of Christ* (see 1 Pet. 1:11)
• *Spirit of Prophecy* (see Rev. 19:10)
• *Spirit of Glory* (see 1 Pet. 4:14)
• *Comforter* (see John 14:26)
• *Eternal Spirit* (see Heb. 9:14)
• *Spirit of Promise* (see Eph. 1:13)
• *The Promise of the Father* (see Luke 24:49)

Third Personality of the Godhead

The Holy Spirit is not a mere "influence." He is not just an amorphous power or a force. He is the third personality of the Godhead. "So there are three witnesses in heaven: the Father, the Word and the Holy Spirit, and these three are One" (1 John 5:7, *AMP*).

Because He is a person, He does things that persons do. He *speaks* (see Acts 13:2), He *works* (see 1 Cor. 12:11), He *teaches* (see John 14:26) and He *guides* (see John 16:13).

As a person with a personality, He possesses a *mind* (the mind of God; see Rom. 8:27), a *will* (the will of God; see 1 Cor. 12:11) and *intelligence* (see Neh. 9:20). The Holy Spirit *loves* (see Rom. 15:30). He can be *grieved* (see Eph. 4:30).

Prophetic Symbols of the Spirit in Scripture

Because He is an invisible spirit, the Bible uses metaphorical symbols to describe the Holy Spirit.

He is compared to a *dove* (see Matt. 3:16), *water* (see John 4:14; 7:38-39), *rain* (see Joel 2:23), *oil* (see Ps. 89:20), and also to *wind* (see John 3:8; Acts 2:2) and *fire* (see Luke 3:16; Isa. 4:4; Acts 2:3).

All of these comparisons tell us something about the nature of the Holy Spirit, and about how He wants to relate to us. That is what He wants to do—relate to the people who have surrendered their lives to the Father in the name of His Son, Jesus.

The Baptism in the Holy Spirit

The experience of the disciples on Pentecost can be our experience today. Here is the account of what happened to them:

> When the Day of Pentecost had fully come, they were all with one accord in one place. And suddenly there came a sound from heaven, as of a rushing mighty wind, and it filled the whole house where they were sitting. Then there appeared to them divided tongues, as of fire, and one sat upon each of them. And they were all filled with the Holy Spirit and began to speak with other tongues, as the Spirit gave them utterance (Acts 2:1-4, *NKJV*).

If you have not yet been filled with the Holy Spirit (or if you are not sure), you can be filled today! Being immersed—baptized—in the Holy Spirit will equip you for living the supernatural life just as it did on the "birthday of the Church" 2,000 years ago. It can happen right where you are as you are reading this. To be filled with the Holy Spirit, you will not need to go to Jerusalem, wait in an upper room, hear wind or see tongues of fire over your head.

But you can expect to see some evidence that He has accepted your invitation to move in.

When Jesus promised the disciples, "you will receive power when the Holy Spirit comes on you; and you will be my witnesses in Jerusalem, and in all Judea and Samaria, and to the ends of the earth" (Acts 1:8), He was speaking not only to those who could hear His voice, but to anyone who would read or hear those words in the future, on down through the centuries. After all, being witnesses "to the ends of the earth" requires more than a handful of disciples whose reach was limited to one part of the globe. So Jesus could have been saying, "You, *too*, [fill in your name], will receive power when the Holy Spirit comes on you."

When you receive spiritual power, that power is one significant piece of evidence of the fullness of the Holy Spirit. When ordinary people suddenly have the ability to speak in languages they did not learn (see Acts 2:4), to heal the sick with their shadows (see Acts 5:15), and so much more, you know that they have been indwelt with supernatural power.

How is this baptism in (or with, or of) the Holy Spirit different from what happens when people are born again? At our conversion, "we were all given the one Spirit to drink" (1 Cor. 12:13). After conversion, "the Spirit of him who raised Jesus from the dead is living in you" (Rom. 8:11). Is that the same as being baptized in the Spirit?

I like Cindy Jacobs's example of the difference between being born again and being baptized or immersed in the Holy Spirit. In her book *The Super-Natural Life: Experiencing the Power of God in Your Everyday Life*, she says that being born again is like when a Coke bottle is tossed into a lake. The bottle is bobbing around on the surface of the lake. It is in the lake, and that is like being converted or born again.

But when the lake water starts to rush into the open bottle, that bottle gets completely filled with water. The bottle is still in the lake, but now the lake is in the bottle too. From the bottle's perspective, the lake water is now not only around it, but also inside it. The bottle is immersed in the lake. That's like being baptized in the Holy Spirit.[1]

To be filled with the Spirit of the living God is to be filled with ever-renewing life that bubbles up with joy. The Spirit of God in you burns away impurities and anoints you with power. The indwelling Holy Spirit fills your heart with love—and besides power, *love* is one of the foremost signs to expect.

When you are baptized in the Holy Spirit, you can expect to be able to exercise one or more of the nine gifts of the Spirit mentioned in 1 Corinthians 12:8-12. This is how the Spirit works in and through the believers He indwells. When you are baptized in the Spirit, you can also expect to see the nine fruit of the Spirit—love, joy, peace, patience, kindness, goodness, faithfulness, gentleness and self-control (the character traits of God; see Galatians 5:22-23)—more prominently in your life.

It is important to *invite the Holy Spirit to fill you*. The rest is up to Him. He will even give you the desire to ask. That's what He did for an Argentinean pastor named Claudio Freidzon, who wrote a book called *Holy Spirit, I Hunger for You*. He wrote: "The year 1992 represented a new period in my ministry. God poured out a saltshaker on my tongue, causing an intense spiritual thirst—a hunger for the Holy Spirit! He not only filled my cup with the Holy Spirit, but He made the Spirit overflow toward others."[2]

Filled and Fulfilled

On Pentecost, the baptism of the Spirit did not happen out of the blue. The disciples had obeyed Jesus, who had spoken with them after His resurrection:

> On one occasion, while he was eating with them, he gave them this command: "Do not leave Jerusalem, but wait for the gift my Father promised, which you have heard me speak about. For John baptized with water, but in a few days you will be baptized with the Holy Spirit" (Acts 1:4-5).

So they were waiting and praying expectantly. They did not know exactly when it would happen, nor did they know exactly what it would mean to be "baptized with the Holy Spirit." On Pentecost, it happened, suddenly. When they were all baptized in the Holy Spirit at the same time, it represented the fulfillment of a long line of prophetic utterances in both the Old and the New Testaments.

Today, our lives are part of that same story line. The promise of the Holy Spirit is a promise for the Church for all ages. Here is just a sampling of scriptural prophecy regarding the filling and overflowing actual presence of the Holy Spirit:

> I will pour out my Spirit on your offspring, and my blessing on your descendants (Isa. 44:3).

I will give you a new heart and put a new spirit
in you; I will remove from you your heart of
stone and give you a heart of flesh (Ezek. 36:26).

Afterward I will pour out My Spirit upon all
flesh; and your sons and your daughters shall
prophesy, your old men shall dream dreams,
your young men shall see visions. Even upon the
menservants and upon the maidservants in
those days will I pour out My Spirit (Joel 2:28-
29, *AMP*).

[John the Baptist:] "I baptize you with water,
but he will baptize you with the Holy Spirit"
(Mark 1:8).

Authority and Power

The main purpose of the baptism in the Holy Spirit is
that we might receive supernatural power. The new birth
gives us the right to be God's children, while the baptism in the Spirit brings us the power to live effective
lives as His children. Being born again gives us an inheritance in the Kingdom of our Father (see Rom. 8:14-17;
Eph. 1). A very important part of that inheritance is the
indwelling presence of His Holy Spirit.

Common Manifestations of the Baptism
in the Holy Spirit
What should we look for as evidence of being baptized
in the Spirit? We can use the account in the book of

Acts as a starting point. When the 120 believers were all filled with the Holy Spirit, everyone, even the strangers in the street, witnessed these manifestations of the "power blast" from heaven:

- the fire of God
- obvious power, beyond human power
- the appearance of drunkenness
- speaking in unknown languages (tongues)
- prophesying
- sudden revelation
- great conviction
- boldness to testify

The people who gathered in the street cried out, "What does this mean?" (Acts 2:12), whereupon Peter boldly stepped forward and preached an amazing sermon that was powerful and completely to the point (see Acts 2:14-36). He explained the unusual manifestations in terms of their prophetic underpinnings, which were very familiar to these Jews. He connected Jesus (who had so recently been crucified) to the events they were witnessing. His preaching was so powerful that the people cried out to Peter and the other apostles standing with him, "Brothers, what shall we do?" (Acts 2:37).

They did not say, "What must we do to be saved?" as so many people add in. They cried out, several thousand of them, just "What shall we do?" They were convicted and desperate. They wanted it all.

Peter told them to repent and get baptized in the name of Jesus for the forgiveness of sins. "And you will receive the gift of the Holy Spirit. The promise is for you and your children and for all who are far off—for all whom the Lord our God will call" (Acts 2:38-39).

Do you see what Peter said? "The promise is for you and your children and for all who are far off." That includes you and me. It includes our children and our grandchildren. It includes anyone who hears the call of God and who responds to it. This supernatural life, this empowering of the Holy Spirit was not only for those who happened to be in Jerusalem that day. It is for everyone, to the farthest corners of the earth, in whatever generation they are born into.

What does the promise include? That everyone, young and old, can receive the same Spirit, the Spirit of the Lord, wisdom, understanding, counsel, might, knowledge, prophecy, glory, comfort, and much more. That sounds like something I want in on!

The Holy Spirit, Key to Living the Christian Life

From every side of the Christian spectrum, men and women of God agree that the Holy Spirit is utterly necessary to living a fully Christian life. You cannot expect to accomplish supernatural feats without supernatural power. Nobody can do it without the Helper. Nobody can fulfill even one of Jesus' commands without the help of the Spirit. Can you do something as "simple" as loving your enemy (see Matt. 5:44) without the empowering love of the Holy Spirit? I can't.

In his book *Experiencing the Spirit: Developing a Living Relationship with the Holy Spirit,* Robert Heidler quotes Jack Hayford (who represents a Pentecostal/charismatic view) and Bill Bright (who represents an evangelical view). Here is how the two of them summarize the vital work of the Holy Spirit:

> *Jack Hayford:* It is the Spirit who keeps the Word alive and progressively being "incarnated" in me. . . . It is the Spirit who infuses prayer and praise with passion and begets vital faith for the supernatural. It is the Spirit who teaches and instructs me so that the mirror of the Word shines Jesus in and crowds sin out; It is the Spirit who brings gifts and giftedness for power ministry to my life . . . and it is the Spirit who will bring love, graciousness and the spirit of unity to my heart so that I not only love the lost and want to see people brought to Christ, but I love all other Christians and refuse to become an instrument of injury to Christ's body—the Church.[3]

> *Bill Bright:* He [the Holy Spirit] guides us (John 16:13), empowers us (Mic. 3:8) and makes us holy (Rom. 15:16), comforts us (John 14:16-26), gives us joy (Rom. 14:17). As our teacher of spiritual truths, the Holy Spirit illuminates our minds with insights into the mind of Christ (1 Cor. 2:12,13) and reveals to us the hidden things of God (Isa. 40:13,14). . . . As you are filled with the Holy Spirit, the Bible becomes alive, prayer becomes vital, your witness becomes effective and obedience becomes a joy. Then, as a result of your obedience in these ar-

eas, your faith grows and you become more mature in your spiritual life.[4]

Filled and Overflowing

Every one of these things provides manifest evidence of a powerful inundation with the Holy Spirit. And the filling continues, overflowing to the world around you.

Outwardly, the invisible presence and power of the Holy Spirit comes down from above, and the believer is surrounded or immersed into His presence and power.

Inwardly, the believer drinks in the Holy Spirit like water until he or she is filled. Eventually, the believer is so completely filled that a river of living water starts to pour forth from the innermost being.

You can have supernatural love. You can have supernatural patience. You can experience supernatural joy—even in the midst of trauma. (And I can testify to that one personally. I am writing this only a few months after my wife of 32 years passed from this life into her heavenly reward.) You will experience supernatural conviction, which is not the same as legalism. Somehow, the light carried by God's Spirit will drive darkness out of your heart, and you will just know what God wants you to do.

With the baptism of the Spirit, you will experience a release of spiritual gifts. The gift of tongues is just a start. Certainly it was the evidence by which the apostles themselves knew they had received their own encounter, and it has become the evidence in the experience of most others. It is not the *only* evidence, but speaking in tongues (speaking in a prayer language that you did not learn previously) is a common outward expression of the presence of the Holy Spirit in someone's life.

How to Be Filled with the Holy Spirit

In the Bible, we see two distinct methods by which the Holy Spirit was imparted to believers: (1) as a Holy Spirit initiative and a human response, as on the day of Pentecost; and (2) through the laying on of hands, as in Acts 8:14-17 (*NKJV*):

> Now when the apostles who were at Jerusalem heard that Samaria had received the word of God, they sent Peter and John to them, who, when they had come down, prayed for them that they might receive the Holy Spirit. For as yet He had fallen upon none of them. They had only been baptized in the name of the Lord Jesus. Then they laid hands on them, and they received the Holy Spirit.

A believer who desires to be filled with the Spirit must only meet certain very basic conditions:

1. Believe that it is God's promise for you today (see Acts 2:39).
2. Prepare your heart through repentance (see Acts 2:38).
3. Ask (see Luke 11:13).
4. Have faith to receive (see John 7:38-39; Gal. 3:2).

Contemporary New Testament Stories

As ongoing proof that the baptism in the Holy Spirit is the key to living the supernatural life, we can find a steady stream of changed lives long after the New Testament was completed. These are people whose lives have been characterized by the "power blasts" of the Spirit.

In my own experience, one of those witnesses is Rodney Howard Browne, the South African evangelist to the United States. Years ago, I remember reading a line like this in one of his books, and it made a huge difference in my approach to the things of the Spirit: "Those whom God is using today—it is not because they are anyone special, but because they have touched God and God has touched them." Browne is just an ordinary, rough kind of a guy. In fact, I call him the Holy Ghost Bulldog. But God uses him mightily, and his life is making a powerful difference in the lives of others.

Charles Finney became a well-known American evangelist in the nineteenth century. This is Finney's own account of being baptized with the Holy Spirit. He had just seen a friend to the door one evening:

> As I closed the door and turned around, my heart seemed to be liquid within me. All my feelings seemed to rise and flow out; and the utterance of my heart was, "I want to pour my whole soul out to God." The rising of my soul was so great that I rushed into the room back of the front office, to pray.
>
> There was no fire [in the fireplace], and no light in the room; nevertheless it appeared to me as if it were perfectly light. As I went in and shut the door after me, it seemed as if I met the Lord Jesus Christ face to face . . . as I would see any other man. He said nothing, but looked at me in

such a manner as to break me right down at His feet. . . . [I]t seemed to me a reality that He stood before me and I fell down at His feet and poured out my soul to Him. I wept like a child. . . . I bathed His feet with my tears.

Finney continued in this state for some time, long enough so that when he returned to the other room, the well-stocked fire in the fireplace had burned low.

[A]s I turned and was about to take a seat by the fire, I received a mighty baptism of the Holy Ghost. . . . The Holy Spirit descended upon me in a manner that seemed to go through me, body and soul. I could feel the impression like a wave of electricity going through and through me. Indeed it seemed to come in waves and waves of liquid love . . . like the very breath of God . . . it seemed to fan me like immense wings.

No words can express the wonderful love that was shed abroad in my heart. I wept aloud with joy and love; and . . . I literally bellowed out the unutterable gushings of my heart. These waves came over me, and over me, and over me one after the other until I recollect I cried out, "I shall die if these waves continue to pass over me. . . . Lord, I cannot bear any more."[5]

Personally, as I began to travel in ministry subsequent to being baptized in the Spirit, I began to experience the gifts of the Spirit, including prophecy. Because I often see visions, I categorize myself as a "seer." Sometimes, I have seen Jesus, as Finney did.

One time, while I was ministering in New York City to a group of church leaders, I could feel the presence of Jesus drawing near. Then my spiritual eyes were opened for a bit and I could see a glimpse of His feet as He walked among the people. Those in the room almost seemed oblivious to His manifested presence. I became desperate for them. I wanted to shake them out of their seeming passivity and exhort them, "Jesus is right here. Somebody just reach out and grab Him!"

These are just a few snapshots from my supernatural photo album. My own Holy Spirit experiences could fill a whole book, and I have written many of them in books. Hundreds of other people have written about their experiences as well. It is easy to find out about other people's experiences of being baptized in the Holy Spirit and of living the supernatural life—just borrow or buy some books or search on the Internet.

His Call Today—Where Is Blind Bartimaeus?

As it was with Charles Finney, and as it was with blind Bartimaeus (see Mark 10:46-52), so the Lord today is looking for people who are hungry and thirsty, who will not hold back but rather cry out with all their hearts, "Have mercy on me, Son of David!" "I must have more of you, Jesus!" We must be willing to cast off the cloak of intimidation and simply come to Him, desperate for His touch.

As we pursue Him, we must encourage each other:

And do not get drunk with wine, for that is dissipation, but be filled with the Spirit, speaking to one another in psalms and hymns and spiritual songs, singing and making melody with your heart to the Lord; always giving thanks for all things in the name of our Lord Jesus Christ to God, even the Father (Eph. 5:18-20, *NASB*).

Review

The glorious baptism of the Holy Spirit is regarded as being a distinct experience from salvation and water baptism. The Word of God declares in John 1:33 that it is the ministry of Christ to baptize the believer in the Holy Spirit. Do you want more of the ministry of Jesus? Then open your heart, ask with faith and receive the empowering of the Holy Spirit.

Be filled with the Holy Spirit, and you will be able to live a supernatural life!

1. What are several of the actions of the Holy Spirit in a person's life, both inward and outward?

2. Does the Holy Spirit always give the same evidence of His presence in a person? Why or why not?

3. What is your own story of being baptized in the Holy Spirit? What evidence of God's supernatural power have you seen in your life?

Part II
It Takes Character

Even though the Holy Spirit often comes suddenly as He did on the day of Pentecost, that does not mean that there are shortcuts to the supernatural life. Just as physical life is a matter of growing steadily and bearing fruit over a long period of time, so is spiritual life. Occasional supernatural *experiences* notwithstanding, living a truly supernatural *life* requires the development of character traits such as faithfulness, patience and balance.

I once heard the fiery British evangelist Leonard Ravenhill say, "With the Spirit only, you will blow up. With the Word only, you will dry up. But with the Spirit and the Word, you will grow up!" He was trying to be light-hearted, but he was absolutely accurate.

There are no shortcuts to the supernatural life because there are no shortcuts to discipleship. And the supernatural life, after all, is a life of discipleship. Remember what Jesus said: "He who does not take his cross and follow after Me is not worthy of Me. He who finds his life will lose it, and he who loses his life for My sake will find it" (Matt. 10:38-39, *NKJV*).

If you want to live a supernatural life, take a deep breath, bend down low and pick up your cross.

Chapter 4

Back to Basics

On one Mother's Day several years ago, I decided to give my late wife, Michal Ann, a very special Mother's Day present. The best gift I could think of was to pray for her.

As I began to pray, my spiritual eyes were opened for a moment. In a vision, over Michal Ann's head, I saw a clear crystal pitcher that was etched with the numbers "9" and "2." The "2" was smaller; the two numbers were in the mathematical configuration of nine to the second power. It resembled the beautiful, etched lead crystal pitcher I had recently brought home from the region of Bohemia in the Czech Republic, which is famous for its crystal.

As I watched the vision, this beautiful pitcher was tipped down, and clear water poured out upon Michal Ann's head. The fluid seemed to go down inside her being. I heard the Holy Spirit say, "I am going to teach you about 'the double.' You have heard how Elisha asked a difficult thing—he asked for a double portion of the anointing that rested upon Elijah, and he received it. We are going for 'the double' this time."

I continued to watch as the water poured into my wife. It seemed that some kind of brown sediment was pushed down deep inside her, and then light brown water began pouring out of her as the clear water kept pouring in from above. The more water that flowed through her, the clearer became the water that flowed out of her. Eventually the water coming out of her was as clear as that going in. Again, I heard the words, "We are going for 'the double' this time—the fullness of character and the fullness of power."

Instantly, I understood that the "nine to the second power" symbol etched on the pitcher signified the joining of the nine fruits of the Holy Spirit (the fullness of character) with the nine gifts of the Spirit (the fullness of power).

This is meant to be true for all of us. Each of us has "brown sediment" inside. If we allow the Holy Spirit to pour through us like a clear river, He will wash out all of the sludge and fill every cranny of our beings with His life. He will continue to pour His living water into each of us to flush away the hurts, bitterness and other debris that we are trying to hide. He is determined to make us into vessels that contain His glory.

In our pursuit of keys to the supernatural life, let's co-operate with the work of the cross in our lives so that we can be true disciples of Jesus, people who have the character to carry those amazing supernatural gifts of God.

This is so simple and yet so profound. The key to living a supernatural life is dying to self and living to God. Maybe it is my age and the things I have gone through, but I am actually beginning to believe that developing a Christlike character is just as much a supernatural miracle as healing a blind person or pulling someone out of a wheelchair. The Holy Spirit won't stop at just a few signs and wonders. He wants to make you all new, through and through.

The key to living a supernatural life is living a cruci-fied life. Living a crucified life has *got* to be supernatural, because everything within my human flesh objects to self-sacrifice. Only by the power of the Holy Spirit— daily—can I take up my cross and live a supernaturally natural life.

A Firm Foundation

Going back to the basics of living the Christian life involves a foundation check.

With any building, the depth and strength of the foundation determines what can be built upon it. There is a fixed relationship between the firmness of the foundation and the size and permanence of the structure that is built upon it.

Psalm 11:3 states, "If the foundations are destroyed, what can the righteous do?" (*NASB*). Ask yourself this question. Whether you are just investigating the Christian life or you are a new believer in Christ or you are someone who has been a true disciple for decades, you will want to make sure that your foundation is rock-solid.

Jesus, the Rock

In Psalm 18:2, King David exclaimed, "The Lord is my rock"! In another psalm, he elaborated:

> My soul finds rest in God alone;
>   my salvation comes from him.
> *He alone is my rock* and my salvation;
>   he is my fortress, I will never be shaken. . . .
> Find rest, O my soul, in God alone;
>   my hope comes from him.

He alone is my rock and my salvation;
   he is my fortress, I will not be shaken.
My salvation and my honor depend on God;
   he is my mighty rock, my refuge (Ps. 62:1-2,5-7,
emphasis added).

Later, the great Isaiah prophesied of Jesus:

So this is what the Sovereign Lord says:
   "See, I lay a stone in Zion,
   a *tested stone,*
   a precious cornerstone for a sure foundation;
   the one who trusts will never be dismayed"
(Isa. 28:16, emphasis added).

Hundreds of years later, quoting Isaiah, both Peter and Paul spoke of Jesus as the cornerstone, the rock who keeps the foundation firm:

You are no longer foreigners and aliens, but fellow citizens with God's people and members of God's household, built on the foundation of the apostles and prophets, with *Christ Jesus himself as the chief cornerstone.* In him the whole building is joined together and rises to become a holy temple in the Lord (Eph. 2:19-21, emphasis added).

For in Scripture it says:

See, I lay a *stone* in Zion,
   a chosen and precious cornerstone,

and the one who trusts in him

will never be put to shame (1 Pet. 2:6, emphasis added).

Luke and Paul used the same metaphor:

He [Jesus] is "the *stone* you builders rejected, which has become the *capstone*." Salvation is found in no one else, for there is no other name under heaven given to men by which we must be saved" (Acts 4:11-12, emphasis added).

For no one can lay any *foundation* other than the one already laid, *which is Jesus Christ* (1 Cor. 13:11, emphasis added).

Building Upon the Foundation

So far, so good. Jesus is our Rock and our firm foundation. But you know that we have got to do more than merely talk about a foundation. We've got to learn how to *build our lives* on Jesus the Rock. We do that by hearing and doing what He tells us to do. Hearing and doing—this, too, is very elementary but critically important. Here's how Jesus described it:

Therefore everyone who hears these words of Mine and acts on them, may be compared to a wise man who built his house on the rock. And the rain fell, and the floods came, and the winds blew and slammed against that house; and yet it did not fall, for it had been founded on the rock.

Everyone who hears these words of Mine and does not act on them, will be like a foolish man who built his house on the sand. The rain fell, and the floods came, and the winds blew and slammed against that house; and it fell—and great was its fall (Matt. 7:24-27, *NASB*).

The rain will fall and the floods will come and the winds will slam against everyone's life, whether or not their lives have been built on the rock. Everyone will get the same storm warnings and the same weather. The difference is in the preparation. Who are the ones who are prepared for anything? The ones who have their lives built on the Rock of Jesus Christ. They are the ones who can endure every test.

Study to Show Yourself Approved

The apostle Paul wrote letters to the young man Timothy, giving him advice about living the supernatural life to which God had called him. He urged him:

Study and be eager and do your utmost to present yourself to God approved (tested by trial), a workman who has no cause to be ashamed, correctly analyzing and accurately dividing [rightly handling and skillfully teaching] the Word of Truth (2 Tim. 2:15, *AMP*).

The Word of God holds the answers for abundant life, and in today's present darkness we should take Paul's advice to Timothy. Every believer needs to know the Word of

God *fully*. To be our best and to use our faith effectively, we must continually "imbibe" the Word of God, becoming intimately familiar with our Bibles. I always say it this way: "The goal is to read your Bible until it reads you."

If you find Bible reading to be a chore, ask the Holy Spirit to enliven it for you. He will. Very often when people are baptized in the Holy Spirit, they notice that the Scriptures "come alive" as never before.

The written Word, after all, is the Living Word. Jesus is called the Word (see John 1:1,14; Rev. 19:13); and if you want a relationship with the Word named Jesus, you must have a relationship with His written Word.

When Jesus was living on earth and teaching His band of disciples, He said as much. Here are His basics for living the supernatural life, His ABCs of discipleship:

> "After a little while the world will no longer see Me, but you will see Me; because I live, you will live also. In that day you will know that I am in My Father, and you in Me, and I in you. He who has My commandments and keeps them is the one who loves Me; and he who loves Me will be loved by My Father, and I will love him and will disclose Myself to him."
>
> Judas (not Iscariot) said to Him, "Lord, what then has happened that You are going to disclose Yourself to us and not to the world?"
>
> Jesus answered and said to him, "If anyone loves Me, he will keep My word; and My Father will love him, and We will come to him and make Our abode with him" (John 14:19-23).

Do you want a revelatory experience? Do you want to live a truly supernatural life? In order to walk it out successfully, you will need to meet certain conditions. In order to keep His Word, you need His Spirit; and in order to receive His Spirit, you need the Word. The Father and the Son come into the life of a disciple and establish their abiding home with him or her through the disciple's obedient response to the Word.

If you are rooted and grounded in the Word, any supernatural experience you may have will be grounded in the truth. As you know, Satan manufactures counterfeit spiritual experiences (see 2 Cor. 11:14; 2 John 1:7). Although he is God's enemy and he is not as great as God, he is a supernatural being. We can easily become confused.

But if we are familiar with the written Word, we can learn to discern. The Bible itself tells us that God speaks through various supernatural means (see Acts 2:17). But it also cautions us that all revelation must be tested by the standards of God's Word (see 1 Thess. 5:19-21; Isa. 8:20; Matt. 24:23-25; and 1 Tim. 4:13).

God has exalted His Word above even His own name (see Ps. 138:2). As God's children, we need to exalt His Word and make it a priority in our lives. By putting the Word first in your life, you will experience far more of God's supernatural life and blessing. The Word tells you who God is and what He has done in you and for you. The Word is full of God's life and power. If you will meditate on it and plant it in your heart, mixing it with active faith in the Living Word, you will begin to experience life and power in a fuller and fuller measure.

How Can You Study the Bible Most Effectively?

You need to study the Bible in order to understand it (see 2 Cor. 1:13-14). *It's not how much you read; it's how much you digest.* Be like a cow; learn to chew and re-chew what you read. To get the most out of it, "ruminate" on it. Digest it so that it becomes part of you. Read it well, so that it may be well with you all the days of your life (see Isa. 34:16).

Here are some practical tips that will help you get the most out of reading the Bible:

1. Read the text in context. Read chapter by chapter, day by day (see Deut. 17:19).

2. Acknowledge Jesus' lordship when you read. Let His truth and light permeate your darkness. Read the Word of God with conviction that it is God's Word historical and God's Word present tense.

3. Read prayerfully and with the Holy Spirit's help. Take note of whatever stands out to you (see Dan. 10:21). Write dates in the margins of your Bible.

4. Mark your Bible, highlighting or underlining in various colors to draw your attention again to those things noted by the Spirit. Those verses will become building blocks for the future development of knowledge and truth in your life.

5. Study certain themes, such as "redemption." As you study, ask yourself: (a) How? (b) When? (c) Where? and (d) Why?

6. Study the lives of important people in the Bible and consider: (a) Why did God choose this person? (b) What did this person do to comply with God's dealing? (c) By what means did God bring this person to His purposes? (d) What lessons can you learn from this person's life that will help you learn faith and patience (see Rom. 15:4; Heb. 6:12)?

7. Using a study Bible and a concordance, and following cross-references, list the many ways particular words are used. Using cross-references will preserve you from a narrow viewpoint, and many times you will find new openings to greater truth.

8. Using a lexicon and a concordance, study the etymology of particular words (the history of the development of the word, the origins of the word in another language such as Greek or Hebrew) and other ways the translated word has been used in Scripture.

Always be ready to enlarge your understanding as more truth becomes clear. Knowledge and doctrine come to us little by little, line upon line:

Whom will he teach knowledge?
And whom will he make to understand the
    message?
Those just weaned from milk?
Those just drawn from the breasts?

For precept must be upon precept, precept upon
  precept,
Line upon line, line upon line,
Here a little, there a little (Isa. 28:9-10, *NKJV*).

As you learn the Word and the ways of God more perfectly, you will be changed and enlarged into His image:
"But we all, with open face beholding as in a glass the glory
of the Lord, are changed into the same image from glory to
glory, even as by the Spirit of the Lord" (2 Cor. 3:18, *KJV*).

Presentation and Revelation

Two of the words that you might want to study in Scripture
are the noun "presentation" and the verb "present." Paul
told the church in Rome: "Therefore I urge you, brethren,
by the mercies of God, to *present* your bodies a living and
holy sacrifice, acceptable to God, which is your spiritual
service of worship" (Rom. 12:1, *NASB*, emphasis added).
The *New International Version* translates the word as "offer."

Earlier in his letter to the Romans, Paul had stated the
obvious, saying that you will become the slave of whatever
or whomever you present yourself to (see Rom. 6:16). If
you present yourself to sin, you become a slave of sin. If you
present yourself to God, you become His willing bondser-
vant, a "slave" of righteousness.

Before we can expect to get further revelation from
God, we must present ourselves to Him more fully.

A Living and Holy Sacrifice

How do we present ourselves to Him? We do it in terms of
our *availability*, our *faithfulness* and our *obedience*.

Availability. Your best ability is your availability to God. Your availability gives God an opportunity to do a miracle through you. All that Isaiah had to offer God was his availability:

> I heard the voice of the Lord saying, "Whom shall I send? And who will go for us?" And I said, "Here am I. Send me!" (Isa. 6:8).

Nobody forced Isaiah to make himself available. "Whom shall I send?" was an open question, not a command. But Isaiah volunteered. He made himself available to the Lord. He presented his time and energy to God.

If you hear God calling, and you respond, "Here I am; send me!" I promise you that God will fill you with His Spirit and He will use you. You don't have to be perfect. Just present yourself to Him. God doesn't seem to require people who are already fixed up and shaped up. In fact, He seems to prefer people who are less that perfect (see 1 Cor. 1:26-30).

Faithfulness. Through your faithfulness, you walk out your availability. This is very basic, but also very important.

If you are not faithful through and through—in the little bitty things as well as the big, sweeping things—you are not really faithful. If your task is setting up the chairs or working in the nursery or running a video camera or lifting someone up in prayer, just keep doing it consistently and well.

It could be as humble as working at Wendy's fast-food restaurant. Before my wife and I had our children, and before she ever had a worldwide humanitarian aid ministry, she made doughnuts and cinnamon rolls. She had to get up early in the morning so she could make them for the local college. Then, after a while, she took a job at Wendy's; it happened to be the first Wendy's that opened in our town. While she worked there, she prayed in tongues. Nobody could hear her. She wasn't trying to be hyper-spiritual. She was just working and praying. Her supervisor was intrigued by her because she emanated some kind of spiritual presence while she was working consistently at her tasks day after day.

She ended up leading her supervisor to the Lord, and I got to water-baptize him. We also got him immersed in the Spirit. It was all because of Michal Ann's faithfulness.

The point is that a person who is faithful in little things will be able to be faithful in big things. If you are faithful as you work for someone else, you will prove that you are ready to handle more (see Luke 16:10-12).

Obedience. Availability and faithfulness go along with obedience. Presenting yourself to God is an act of obedience.

Obedience is not coercion; it is not a chore. Rather, obedience is an act of gratitude toward God. It is not works performance, and you don't obey in order to twist God's arm.

The writer William A. Ward penned this maxim: "Every great person has learned how to obey, whom to obey and when to obey." I think it should be part of every "successful living" seminar in the business world, and also in the Church. As disciples of Jesus, our obedience centers on Him.

Availability and faithfulness nudge open the door to revelation. Obedience opens it the rest of the way. Paul poses an interesting question: "Does God give you his Spirit and work miracles among you because you observe the law, or because you believe what you heard?" (Gal. 3:5). In other words, if you have presented yourself to God and have exercised obedient faith, it proves that you belong to Him—and you will see supernatural manifestations of His presence.

> [You] were chosen and foreknown by God the Father and consecrated (sanctified, made holy) by the Spirit to be obedient to Jesus Christ (the Messiah) and to be sprinkled with [His] blood: May grace (spiritual blessing) and peace be given you in increasing abundance [that spiritual peace to be realized in and through Christ, freedom from fears, agitating passions, and moral conflicts] (1 Pet. 1:2, *AMP*).

Jesus was obedient, and we are supposed to model ourselves on His example. Jesus accomplished the work His Father gave Him to do (see John 17:4). He pleased the Father by always doing His will (see John 4:34; 5:30; 6:38). If we intend to live on this earth as He did, our lives must be marked by faithful and faith-filled obedience. Then it won't matter if we are assigned to clean the toilets or preach to 250,000 people—the reward will be the same.

Spiritual Eyes Enlightened

By presenting yourself to God, you become a candidate for revelation from Him. The eyes of your heart become enlightened as you step into a new level of the supernaturally abundant life to which you have been called. Here's Paul again:

> I pray also that the eyes of your heart may be enlightened in order that you may know the hope to which he has called you, the riches of his glorious inheritance in the saints, and his incomparably great power for us who believe (Eph. 1:18-19).

As you and I present ourselves to God, we can ask Him for a revelation concerning (1) the *will* of God, (2) the *compassion* of God and (3) the *victory* of God. He will give us the revelation we need, personally tailored to each of us.

What is His will for you? Because you are a carrier of the Spirit of Jesus, God's will for you will be like His expressed will for His Son (see Luke 4:18-19). He will want to use you to bring the Kingdom wherever you go. The kingdom of God comes with loving compassion. It conquers darkness with victorious light.

Ready to Do His Bidding

As I was preparing this chapter, I had a little encounter that provides a good example of how the Holy Spirit can use someone in an ordinary situation.

I was speaking at a church, and between sessions, I was getting a meal at an Olive Garden restaurant. As my server came up to me, I felt a little tug inside my spirit. I felt the love of the Father for this young man, and I gave him a prophetic word of encouragement: "You really are faithful. God is going to reward your faithfulness. You

have got a pastoral call on your life. In fact, your wife"—
I sincerely hoped he was married—"is a real sparkplug,
and her prayers are going to help propel you forward into
your next place in God."

Of course the guy was astonished. He had no idea
who I was, and I did not know him.

I asked, "Is your wife around?"

He said, "Yes, she works here also! I'll go get her. She
really needs to hear what you just said." It ended up that
this guy was a youth pastor, but he was working full-time
at Olive Garden, and so was his wife. That word of encouragement kept them going faithfully. It helped them
know that God was with them.

Thy Kingdom Come
As we faithfully do our ordinary daily activities with humble and grateful hearts, our goal is to live a supernaturally
natural life as citizens of the kingdom of God. Let us never
forget about the basic, foundational, operational truths
about discipleship in the Kingdom; but let us also not be
afraid to ask God for "the double," as I prayed for my wife.

*Lord, pour the crystal-clear living water of Your Spirit over us
and through us. May our spirits and souls be washed clean. May
we drink in the clarity of both the written Word and the revelatory
Word, and may we present ourselves as living sacrifices to You.*

Review

We have to grow into the supernatural life, always looking for ways to nourish our spirits with the living Word,
and always ready to obey whatever He tells us to do.

Supernatural living is not only—or even mostly—miracles and healings and other supernatural manifestations. It consists largely of discipleship, growth in godly character traits and obedience to the will of God.

1. Why do I say that there are no shortcuts to living a supernatural life?

2. As you read this chapter, did you do a "foundation check" of yourself? What potential weak places or cracks did you find? What have you decided to do about them?

3. After reading this chapter, what additional ways could you present yourself to the Lord as a living sacrifice?

Chapter 5

No Shortcuts

Over the years, the Church has had two types of ministries: "shooting star" ministries and "North Star" ministries.

Shooting stars burst upon the scene in a flash, rise fast and blaze bright. For a short time, they burn furiously, drawing much attention to themselves. They are brilliant for the moment, but they don't last long. All too quickly, they fade from existence, usually through moral failure or some other fatal character flaw.

North Star ministries, however, are like their namesake, the North Star. They are stable and consistent. They may not be very flashy, but they can give guidance to one generation after another on the seas of uncertainty, and they can do so without wavering, flickering out or becoming obliterated with clouds of sin. They are guiding lights in the darkness.

People with a shooting star ministry seek only "the anointing." They go for the fullness of God's power without waiting for the development of godly character and without learning discernment about the wisdom of God. They don't have the patience to grow in maturity, slowly but steadily, through experience and all of the countless small acts of obedience and faithfulness. Shooting starts pay virtually nothing up front, but they pay dearly in the end.

People with a North Star ministry take the higher road. This road has a high personal cost, and it has no shortcuts. The people who travel this road pay the cost of discipleship by taking up their cross daily, following Jesus' commands and obeying the Holy Spirit, one painful step after another. They have submitted themselves to God's will and His Word, and that is how they have become conformed to His image. They have developed the character to carry the gifts that God has given them.

I want to be a North Star, don't you? I want to kiss the cross and come away with a mouthful of splinters! I do not want to be a flash in the pan. I want to become fully mature and bear lasting fruit for the Kingdom. When I finish my course, I want to hear His words of commendation.

The truly supernatural life, as I said in the previous chapter, must be built on a firm foundation. We need to explore the matter of holiness and personal character a little more in depth.

Living the Sermon on the Mount

Both my late wife and I have had some amazing dream experiences. As I have tried to better understand how God speaks to His people through dreams, I have come to realize that the importance of a dream does not depend upon its length. In fact, some of the most meaningful dreams I have had have been the shortest ones.

For example, in the fall of 2007, I dreamed that an old man appeared to me. With rugged features and a clear, raspy voice, I heard him say, "You are never too old for the

Sermon on the Mount." I woke up from that simple dream with those words ringing deep inside, and I decided to review what Jesus said, which has been recorded for us in chapters 5, 6, and 7 of Matthew's Gospel.

The most famous sermon of all time begins with the eight Beatitudes, which go from "Blessed are the poor in spirit" (Matt. 5:3) to "Blessed are those who are persecuted because of righteousness" (Matt. 5:10). (I like the way the *Amplified Bible* expands upon them. For example, the first beatitude reads, "Blessed [happy, to be envied, and spiritually prosperous—with life-joy and satisfaction in God's favor and salvation, regardless of their outward conditions] are the poor in spirit [the humble, who rate themselves insignificant], for theirs is the kingdom of heaven!")

Jesus moves on to tell His listeners how they are like "salt" and "the light of the world" (see Matt. 5:13-16). He mentions that He is the fulfillment of the Old Testament Law, and He tells the people that they should fulfill it too: "I tell you that unless your righteousness surpasses that of the Pharisees and the teachers of the law, you will certainly not enter the kingdom of heaven" (Matt. 5:20).

He expands upon the meaning of the Old Testament Law, explaining that it is not enough to refrain from murder or adultery, but that His followers must refrain even from *thoughts* that are murderously angry or full of lust (see Matt. 5:21-32). The Lord Jesus goes on to forbid the use of oaths and to urge His listeners to "go the second mile," even with their enemies (see Matt. 5:33-42). Then, speaking of enemies, He says, "I tell you: Love your enemies and pray for those who persecute you," and "Be perfect, therefore, as your heavenly Father is perfect" (Matt. 5:44,48).

Are you beginning to see, as I did, that the reason no-body is ever too old for the Sermon on the Mount is that it takes a lifetime of living in the supernatural power of the Holy Spirit to even begin to fulfill Jesus' commands? "Be perfect"!

That's not the end yet . . . far from it. Jesus was just getting warmed up. He moved on to talk about giving charitable gifts anonymously; in fact, not letting "your left hand know what your right hand is doing" (Matt. 6:3). Not only are we supposed to give charitable gifts without caring about what other people think, but we are also supposed to pray and fast that way too (see Matt. 6:5-18). He included the model for prayer, which we now call the Lord's Prayer (see Matt. 6:9-13), and He made a special point of talking about the importance of forgiveness: "For if you forgive men when they sin against you, your heavenly Father will also forgive you. But if you do not forgive men their sins, your Father will not forgive your sins" (Matt. 6:14-15).

Following the same line of thinking, He talked about laying up treasures in heaven; the way a person's eye is the "lamp" of his body; and about how nobody can serve both God and mammon (money) (see Matt. 6:19-24).

Then he launched into a message about not worrying (see Matt. 6:25-34), followed by a strong word about not judging other people (see Matt. 7:1-6). In case it wasn't clear enough by now, the Lord Jesus talked about the "nar-row way" (see Matt. 7:13-14), and the importance of keep-ing on asking, seeking and knocking until you get the answers you need (see Matt. 7:7-12).

He threw in a strongly worded caution about false prophets, people who are like wolves in sheep's clothing (see Matt. 7:15-20), and then, wrapping up the sermon, the Lord Jesus warned:

> Not everyone who says to me, "Lord, Lord," will enter the kingdom of heaven, but only he who does the will of my Father who is in heaven. Many will say to me on that day, "Lord, Lord, did we not prophesy in your name, and in your name drive out demons and perform many miracles?" Then I will tell them plainly, "I never knew you. Away from me, you evildoers!" (Matt. 7:21-23).

Clearly, we have a lifetime of growing to do. It is the shooting stars who will look for the shortcuts, saying, "Lord! Lord!" but it is the steady North Stars who will do the will of the Father in heaven. We need all the Holy Spirit-supplied help we can get to become North Star believers!

Listening, Waiting and Watching

To grow up spiritually sturdy and healthy, we must be willing to set aside our impatience. We must accept the wisdom of the proverb writer, who recorded the following words:

> Now then, my sons, listen to me;
>   blessed are those who keep my ways.
> *Listen* to my instruction and be wise;
>   do not ignore it.
> Blessed is the man who listens to me,
>   *watching* daily at my doors,
>   *waiting* at my doorway.

> For whoever finds me finds life
> > and receives favor from the Lord.
> But whoever fails to find me harms himself;
> > all who hate me love death (Prov. 8:32-36,
> emphasis added).

The three italicized words are in the present continuous tense. The action is ongoing; it has not ended. It's not "Blessed is the man who once heard my voice," but rather "Blessed is the man who is listening to me continuously," the one who listens and keeps on listening. The man who watches and keeps on watching. The one who waits and keeps on waiting patiently, awake and alert.

The man who does these three things is blessed because he finds God Himself, and in finding God, he finds true, supernatural life. He (or she) who listens, watches and waits—tirelessly and faithfully—will be in a position to receive the fullness of God's life. That's what I want. How about you?

That is what Joshua wanted, and he modeled for us listening, watching and waiting when he lingered at the entrance of the tent of meeting. The other people stayed at their own tents, but young Joshua waited expectantly until Moses emerged from his encounters with God. Joshua was always the first one to see the reflection of God's glory on Moses' countenance (see Exod. 33:7-11).

David, too, knew the art of listening, watching and waiting at the threshold of the door of the house of God. In one of his best-known psalms, he wrote:

> Better is one day in your courts
> > than a thousand elsewhere;

I would rather be a doorkeeper in the house
of my God
     than dwell in the tents of the wicked.
For the Lord God is a sun and shield;
     the Lord bestows favor and honor;
     no good thing does he withhold
     from those whose walk is blameless
(Ps. 84:10-11).

David became a prototype for us. Because of Jesus, we have been made kings in the Kingdom. All of us are prophets and priests, offering up unlimited worship to the One who saved us. David was a king. He was a prophet. He was a priest. He established the tabernacle with constant worship. He started out as one who listened, watched and waited at God's threshold, and he ended up with more honor than any other king.

Listen

The best way to begin to learn the art of listening to God is to read about it in the Word and to take the Word personally. For example, here is one of my favorite passages:

The Lord God has given Me the tongue of disciples,
     That I may know how to sustain the weary
     one with a word
     He awakens Me morning by morning,
     He awakens My ear to listen as a disciple.
The Lord God has opened My ear;
     And I was not disobedient
     Nor did I turn back (Isa. 50:4-5, *NASB*).

You can pray these verses over your own life, asking to be given a listening ear.

The well-known story of the cleansing of the Temple ends with a few easily missed words about listening: "Every day he was teaching at the temple . . . [and] all the people hung on his words" (Luke 19:47-48). He is still teaching daily in the temple—in your temple. Are you hanging on His words?

Certainly none of us will "hear" in exactly the same way; that is part of the beauty of our listening to God. I have written several books about the many ways we hear the voice of God, including one of the other books in this series, *The Beginner's Guide to Hearing God*. As you listen for His voice, you will learn how best to "tune in." You may not ever hear an actual voice. Often what you will "hear" is more like a fleeting thought that somehow just has the stamp of God on it. Sometimes I wake up in the morning with the words to a song running through my head. That is God talking to me. Sometimes I see pictures in my mind's eye—visions—or I have "visions in the night," which means I have dreams. Did you know that you can listen to a vision? Well, you can. You just pay attention to what the pictures are communicating to you.

Now several of the disciples did hear the actual voice of the Father when they were on the Mount of Transfiguration (see Mark 9:7-8). They heard, "This is My beloved Son, listen to Him!" The Father was telling them to listen and keep listening to the voice of Jesus. They, and we, need to keep listening, even though Jesus has ascended to heaven. When He left His disciples, He sent the Holy Spirit, and the Spirit helps us to listen to God as He helped them.

Obstacles to Hearing God's Voice

If God is always speaking, and if He has given us His Spirit to help us listen, why do so many Christians today fail to hear from God on a regular (even daily) basis? I have identified seven reasons why believers' spiritual ears have been stopped:

1. Lack of faith to believe that hearing from God is for today (in other words, a belief in cessationism; more about this in chapter 11)

2. Lack of commitment to Jesus Christ as Lord

3. The presence of unconfessed sin and a "double standard" lifestyle

4. Ignorance of the scriptural evidence of every believer's privilege to hear from God personally

5. Lack of teaching on how to pursue such a listening-prayer experience

6. Fear of being called a religious fanatic or even mentally ill

7. Fear of becoming open to the wrong spirits or being led astray by the enemy

It is my hope that this book and others with a similar message will help people overcome all obstacles to hearing the voice of God.

Is God Speaking to You?

If you can respond to the following statements affirmatively, then rest assured that God *is* speaking to you and that you are hearing Him:

- If what you hear helps you fear God and walk in holiness, then you have heard the Lord (see Job 28:28).

- If what you hear makes faith rise up inside, then you have heard the Lord (see Prov. 4:7).

- If the actions that result from following what you hear are full of spiritual fruit (purity, peace, gentleness, mercy, courtesy, good deeds, sincerity), then you have heard the Lord (see Jas. 3:17).

- If what you hear strengthens you with "all power according to his glorious might so that you may have great endurance and patience," and joy, then you have heard the Lord (see Col. 1:11-12).

I'll give you one more indicator of whether or not you have been hearing God: Almost always, He will not tell you to do something that you cannot accomplish without His help! It is a "God thing" all the way. You need to keep hearing Him—continuously—in order to live a truly supernatural life.

Wait

As if to underline the idea that there are no shortcuts in the Kingdom, Isaiah wrote about the importance of *waiting* for God—as, in fact, He waits for us:

> Therefore *the Lord will wait,* that He may be gracious to you; and therefore He will be exalted, that He may have mercy on you. For the Lord is a God of justice; *blessed are all those who wait* for Him (Isa. 30:18, *NKJV*, emphasis added).

God is waiting and longing to show mercy on us and to render justice. Therefore, the better we are able to wait for Him to act, the more blessing we will receive. He is not waiting with a clenched fist, ready to punish. No, He is waiting with an open hand of blessing to receive us.

As Andrew Murray put it in his book *Waiting on God*:

We must not only think of our waiting upon God, but also of what is more wonderful still, of God's waiting upon us. The vision of Him waiting on us will give new impulse and inspiration to our waiting upon Him. It will give us an unspeakable confidence that our waiting cannot be in vain. . . .

Look up and see the great God upon His throne. He is love—an unceasing and inexpressible desire to communicate His own goodness and blessedness to all His creatures. He longs and delights to bless. He has inconceivably glorious purposes concerning every one of His children, by the power of His holy Spirit. . . . He waits with all the longings of a father's heart. . . .

If you ask: How is it, if He waits to be gracious, that even after I come and wait upon Him, He does not give the help I seek, but waits on longer and longer?. . . God is a wise husbandman, [and He knows that] waiting in the sunshine of His love is what will ripen the soul for His blessing. Waiting under the cloud of trial . . . is as needful. Be assured that if God waits longer than you could wish, it is only to make the blessing doubly precious. . . .

The giver is more than the gift; God is more than the blessing; and, our being kept waiting on Him is [the] only way for our learning to find our life and joy in Himself. . . .

God cannot do His work without His and our waiting His time. Let waiting be our work, as it is His. And, if His waiting is nothing but goodness and graciousness, let ours be nothing but a rejoicing in that goodness, and confident expectancy of that grace.[1]

Watch

"Watching" is a combination of waiting and listening. It is both a gift to be activated and an art to be learned. Watching requires a blend, therefore, of both spiritual gifting and character development.

Those who watch will always be, like watchmen who guarded ancient cities, waiting, looking and listening. The prophet Habakkuk wrote:

> I will stand on my guard post
> And station myself on the rampart;
> And I will keep watch to see what He will speak
>   to me,
> And how I may reply when I am reproved (Hab.
>   2:1, *NASB*).

Habakkuk had the inner attitude of a watchman, which was the key to unlocking his ability to hear and see in the Spirit. Like all guard-watchmen, he was expected to perform two primary tasks:

1. To guard the city against enemies, to resist enemy incursions and to warn the people of dangers

2. To receive ambassadors, to permit them to enter the city

As Spirit-filled believers, you and I are called to "watch duty." Our assigned position on the "wall" in the Kingdom will be perfectly suited to our temperament and circumstances. Years ago, my family lived in a subdivision, and there was a sign at the entrance that said, "This neighborhood is under surveillance watch." I thought that was an accurate prophetic statement because that is what is supposed to happen. We are supposed to be disciples who have our ears open, listening daily and watching at God's doorpost, with a responsibility of stewardship for what comes in and out of our domain. The watchmen are the doorkeepers. They are given the keys to the city or the house. They have the delegated authority to bind or loose, to capture or to permit.

When Jesus was in agony in the Garden of Gethsemane, His band of disciples fell asleep nearby. He woke them up and reprimanded them, saying, "Could you men not keep watch with me for one hour?" (Matt. 26:40). He had not told them to stay awake to pray, only to stay alert and *watch*. His words had been "Sit here while I go over there and pray" (Matt. 26:36).

In many ways, that is all He wants us to do too. Even for that, we need the help of the Holy Spirit. We do not want to receive the Lord's rebuke, nor do we want to suffer the consequences of allowing the enemy to infiltrate or attack (see Ezek. 33:6).

Let us "recalibrate" and resume our long, slow, steady journey of faith, listening attentively for God's voice, waiting faithfully for His blessings and watching the whole time.

Review

The supernatural life does not include shortcuts. In a very real sense, it is both a gift and a growth process. Are you up for it?

1. What is the difference between a shooting-star life and a North Star life?

2. Why must listening, waiting and watching be present and continuous in our lives?

3. What are some of the connections between listening, waiting and watching? Are these passive or active approaches to living the supernatural life?

Chapter 6

Naturally Supernatural

Many people think they have some idea of where they are going. They have their future more or less mapped out for the next few years. Family. Career. Ministry. They may feel that their plans are God-directed, and they may be right.

But I don't think I know anymore. Apart from my final destination, heaven, I am not so sure where the wind of the Spirit will blow me. "The wind blows where it wishes and you hear the sound of it, but do not know where it comes from and where it is going; so is everyone who is born of the Spirit" (John 3:8, *NASB*).

The Proverbs writer captured it well: "The mind of man plans his way, but the Lord directs his steps" (Prov. 16:9, *NASB*). And the Lord is like the wind, purposeful but (from my human point of view) unpredictable.

In order to become naturally supernatural, we need to understand a few things about the wind. First of all, you cannot see it. It is invisible. You can observe its effects, but you cannot see the wind itself. You can, however, hear and feel the wind. Yet even by hearing and feeling it, still you cannot predict where it came from or where it is going.

The wind can be gentle or it can be terrifyingly powerful. Most of the time, even in very windy places, it is possible to harness its power. People use sails and windmills and other devices to take advantage of the power of the wind. I have an old, dilapidated windmill on my property that came from my parents' house. It is not very pretty, but it was my father's windmill, and I cherish it. For me, it has become a prophetic symbol of what I want my life to be like. I want to catch the wind. I want to point in the direction the wind is coming from. I want the wind of the Spirit to be funneled into me so that I can do His work with His power.

In order to live supernaturally, each of us needs to learn to go with the flow of the wind of the Spirit. However, we cannot merely let the wind drive us straight before it. We need to learn how to harness the wind-power. The better we understand the ways of the wind, the more comfortable we will become with the "windy" environment we live in.

The Lost Art of Tacking

I know more about windmills than I do about sailing, but I do know one thing about sailing—you cannot let the wind simply drive you in one direction. In fact, many times, the best way to reach your destination is not to head straight for it—it is to "tack," or shift from one side to the other, zig-zagging across the water to reach your goal.

You may think that the shortest distance between two points is a straight line. But remember, there are no shortcuts with God. You need to hoist your sail up into the headwind and catch it. But then you must reposition it, over and over, essentially sailing into it. To get to your appointed destination, you must learn to angle and re-angle yourself back and forth, and this will help you continue to progress in a forward motion.

Thus it is in the life with God. You angle this way and then you angle that way. You sail with His wind carrying you, learning to shift your position when necessary to stay the course. You do cede control to the wind, but only within the context of the principles you have learned from others and from personal experience, so that you can keep yourself from capsizing.

With the supernatural life, just as it is in sailing, you can't tell if the wind is going to keep blowing in the same direction. It just blows (or not) and you respond accordingly. You can't ask it questions such as "Where are you coming from?" or "Why are you blowing this way?" You just have to take a reading of the current situation and figure out how best to set sail.

The True Supernatural Is Always Personal

Talking about sailing in the wind of the Spirit makes it sound in a way as if the supernatural life is a big guessing and skill game. On the contrary, it is a relationship, and therefore it is always very personal. In fact, one of the ways you can tell that you may be slipping into the wrong kind of supernatural realm, the dark kind, is that it just begins to seem detached from a relationship and devoid of love. The true supernatural life always has a very personal impetus.

Because supernatural life is personal, you don't have to be a spiritual superstar. God delights to employ ordinary, everyday folks for His most important work. He always has and He always will. As my wife used to say, "God is an equal-opportunity employer."

By setting our sails and capturing His wind, you and I can become carriers of God's anointing. Propelled into action by the supernatural flow of the Spirit, we are able to go places we never thought we could go.

The flow of the Holy Spirit gives you an insight into someone's need and enables you to understand that person's heartaches. Your heart is moved with compassion. As you pray about what He has revealed to you, He will give you the wisdom you need. He will show you where to go and how to tack, one repositioning after another, to get there.

The more you do this, the more it becomes like a dance and the better you get at it. He will often surprise you, but you will be delighted. More and more, like a good dancing partner, you will begin to become conformed to the One who is your partner. Over time, you will reflect His image.

Walking in the supernatural life, you will be clothed with love, purity, holiness, tenderheartedness, mercy, kindness, humility, gentleness, patience, endurance, and more. These will come from deep within you, where the Holy Spirit resides. Living out of your close relationship with Him, you will become more flexible, less subject to your need for human control, more dependent on Him and less dependent upon your own resources.

You will live the supernatural life naturally, wherever you go. Driving on the highway, waiting in an airport, eating in a restaurant, working in your garden, putting your kids to bed at night—anywhere and everywhere you go, you can allow His life to shine. You, an everyday person, will be living a supernatural lifestyle.

It takes *character* to live a consistently supernatural life. The supernatural Holy Spirit will help you become a sanctified person—someone who has been washed clean so many times that you reflect God's character. He will help you become so secure in your Kingdom identity that you will not jump to mimic what others do, nor will you need a platform from which to perform supernatural works. You will find that He will use you often, the more so as you learn to move in His anointing power.

Moving in the Anointing

In July 1983, the Lord spoke to me and said, "Five minutes of anointed prayer through you will do more than five hours of counseling as you have done in the past."

He wasn't saying that counseling was worthless. He was simply presenting a principle to me. He was saying that anything that He anoints is more powerful, more efficient and more effective than the same thing without His anointing. His suggestion sounded good to me. I knew I could use the extra 4 hours and 55 minutes!

I began to learn more about what it meant to "move in the anointing" of the Holy Spirit. Not surprisingly, one of the first things I discovered was that moving in the anointing was a lot like sailing in the wind. I had to learn to read the signs He would give me and act accordingly. I learned that He moved in many ways, as William Cowper put it in the words to his famous hymn:

> God moves in a mysterious way
>   His wonders to perform;
> He plants his footsteps in the sea,
>   And rides upon the storm.[1]

I learned that there are options to choose from. As you learn to move in the anointing, you need to know when to jump in and flow and when to pull back and wait. You need to learn dependency and sensitivity to the Holy Spirit. Sometimes it will be exciting, and sometimes it will not. Sometimes you will experience supernatural manifestations and sometimes you will be operating purely on the basis of faith in the truth.

I found out that you can pray at least three divergent ways when you minister in the anointing of the Spirit:

1. *You can pray by what you see with your natural eyes.* You may call forth the Holy Spirit to be released upon a person and then you pray to bless what you observe the Father is doing. All you can see are the natural effects upon a person as the Holy Spirit moves. For example, the person may tremble or cry or receive a sudden insight.

2. *You can pray by what you see with your spiritual eyes.* As you pray, you may see mental pictures, visions or images. You may sense something—you will "just know it." You then invoke the Lord's presence on what you perceive that He wants to do. This is often called revelatory prayer.

3. *You can pray by faith.* You can pray for people because the Bible tells you to do it. Although you may not feel or sense anything, and the person you are praying for may not demonstrate any emotion or movement, you simply step out and act in raw obedience to the Scriptures. Because the Word says you shall lay hands on the sick and they shall recover, you just do it by obedience.

All of these ways of ministering require faith, and they can feel risky. To have that faith, you must have a vital relationship with the Father and Son, through the Holy Spirit, and it is helpful to know that you will be able to choose from various options when responding to the wind of the Spirit.

Compassion and Kindness

As you learn to tell when the wind of the Spirit is propelling you to do something, be sure to look to see if your heart is full of compassion and kindness. Compassion is one of the hallmarks of the Spirit of Jesus in you. When He is using you to reach out in some way, you are allowing His compassion and kindness to pour out of you. Your part is to stay close to Him and be willing to spread His love around.

This aspect of the supernatural lifestyle often has been ignored in favor of the splashy, headline-grabbing exploits of believers who are in the public eye. But love should undergird everything that a Spirit-filled believer does, whether out in public arenas or hidden in private homes.

Some years ago, early in the morning, the Spirit of God spoke to me. His words were not earth shattering, but they have remained with me to this day. He said, simply, "I will have a revival of kindness."

Compassion and kindness. We need them much more desperately than we need more religious churchianity or charismatic hype. Instead of "random acts of kindness," ours can be *intentional* acts of kindness, performed by ordinary believers who happen to be filled with the Spirit of God and who happen to listen and obey when *His* intention is to love someone.

Who knows, you might find yourself giving someone a word of encouragement or an anonymous gift. You might simply be a good listener when someone wants to talk to you. You might feel inspired to give an unusually good tip to a server in a restaurant—one who does not deserve it. In a line of cars at a fast-food drive-thru, you may feel led to pay not only for your own order but also for the order of the car behind you. In the supermarket, at the bank, or at the barbershop, you might surrender your place in line to someone who seems to be in a hurry. You might ask people if you could pray for them, right on the spot.

A next-generation friend of mine named Munday Martin started a ministry called Contagious Love International.[2] For a couple of years, we called people from August 1 to August 21 to join with us in "fasting from our comfort zones." People stepped outside of their self-identified limits for 21 days, looking for where the Spirit would have them spread a little supernatural love. Sometimes it felt a little risky, because we were "fasting" from the tendency to retreat into our passive comfort zones.

We wanted to bring Martha and Mary together (see Luke 10:38-42). We called it Twenty-One Jump Street, because we wanted to jump to the streets. Munday hopes that others will now pick up the ball and fast from their ungodly comfort zones as well!

Trying on Shoes and Hats

God will help you figure out what kind of an anointing to look for. Here's how He helped me.

Years ago, as I was learning how to move in the Spirit, I used to see visions of shoes. These were shoes of very specific descriptions, and they matched the actual shoes of people I knew. So when I was in a ministry situation, and I saw a vision of some shoes, I could figure out that I was about to flow in an anointing that was like that of the owner of those shoes.

For instance, I had spent a lot of time with healing evangelist Mahesh Chavda, and I knew that he always wore black dress shoes. So when I saw black dress shoes, I knew that people were going to fall down like dominoes when I prayed for them and that many of them would be healed. If I saw Bob Jones's gray Hush Puppies, I knew I was going to start receiving a prophetic download and that I would be operating in a "seer anointing." When I saw John Wimber's shoes, I knew that I could expect to usher in the manifest presence of God and that it would fill the room.

I thought I had this all figured out, and then the Holy Spirit surprised me. I was preaching to about 4,000 people in Kansas City. I preached everything I knew, and I preached stuff I didn't know. After preaching for almost two straight hours, I suddenly saw (in the seer anointing) a pair of shoes resting on the edge of the platform. I didn't recognize those shoes. They didn't look like the other ones.

I did something new. I walked over to the edge of the platform and I slipped my feet into those shoes. Nobody else could tell quite what I was doing, because they couldn't see the shoes in the spirit realm. All they could see was me teetering on the edge of the platform. It was a prophetic act—I had to be "on the edge." I had to get into an uncomfortable position in order to put on what turned out to be my *own* shoes that day. Starting that day, I began to be able to minister in my own anointing after having ministered faithfully in the anointing of others. My own anointing had to do with calling down the "burden of the Lord."

Right then, in a half-second, without any teaching from me about travailing or sobbing in prayer, 4,000 people were released into loud weeping en masse. Then I called it to lift, and it lifted. Four times. I called for four burdens to be released that day—for the abortion issue, for Israel and for two more. Each time, all of the people would be thrown into gut-wrenching crying out to God, and then when I would ask for it to lift, it would.

Since then, that particular anointing has been distinctive to James W. Goll, and now to many others as well. After learning to flow with the Holy Spirit by trying on many different shoes (or "hats," to use the standard analogy), eventually I tried on the ones with the best "fit."

The same thing can happen for you. Try on many different shoes or hats of the anointing as you learn to flow with Him. Eventually there will be a time in your life when you will know what you can best serve up to the

Body of Christ. You will learn which special gifting best fits you. When you are wearing that hat, you will be able to flow in the deepest anointing and greatest grace as you minister to others.

Wisdom About Moving in the Anointing

Mahesh Chavda compares the anointing to getting into a scuba diving suit, which is like a second skin. You recognize that it's not you. It's not about you; it is about Jesus Christ. You are stepping into Him and He is clothing you with Himself (see John 15). The main thing to learn about the anointing is that *the anointing is not you.*

The anointing is simple. It is a relationship, remember. It involves asking the Holy Spirit questions: What is this? Do I say it? What now? Where should I go next? To move in the anointing, you need to *ask questions constantly.*

Faithfulness is a major key to walking out your desire to see salvation, healing, deliverance and more take place. *Be faithful in the little and more will come.*

Sometimes the anointing will lift. Do not try to keep it on you by pretending you still have it. Trying to execute the same maneuvers without the Spirit's power will be like scuba diving without a suit. Instead, when you sense that the anointing seems to be lifting, humble yourself before God and ask for fresh grace. *Humility is the key to regaining His presence in anointing.*

How Does the Anointing Increase?

Once you decide to go sailing with the Holy Spirit, how can you make sure that you "stay the course with force"? For starters, be sure not to go sailing or riding off like a lone ranger. Hang out with people who love the anointing and who inhabit a faith-saturated environment. Observe how others operate. Watch and learn from people who know the ways of the Lord.

As John Wimber used to say, just "do the stuff." With persistence and old-fashioned *faithfulness*, keep listening to the Spirit and doing what the Father is doing. To the best of your ability, keep learning as you go. Keep on studying the Word. Keep on praying God's promises back to Him. Keep on hungering and thirsting after His presence. Remember "that He is a rewarder of those who diligently seek Him" (Heb. 11:6, *NKJV*).

Don't forget the time-honored keys of *fasting* and *worship*. Charles Finney, the great nineteenth-century revivalist, whom I mentioned in chapter 3, would go into times of fasting when he felt the presence of God subside. He would fast to call forth the tangible anointing. We can do the same. We can also launch into worship and praise. God is enthroned on the praises of His people (see Ps. 22:3), and His presence will always abide more heavily in an atmosphere of praiseful worship. Author and Bible teacher Bob Mumford once said, "I give the trophies I have received during the course of the day back to the Lord at the end of the day and worship Him with them." Thanksgiving is the track that carries the mighty payload of faith.

There is no substitute for *faith* as you move in the anointing of the Spirit. Remember (I am sure that you have heard this before), the word "faith" is spelled R-I-S-K. Sometimes you will need to teeter on the edge of a platform as I did. Sometimes you will need to call forth a demonstration of His overpowering presence, as Elijah did (see 1 Kings 18). Even if you are the most comfortable with Jesus as a gentle Shepherd, you may need to step out and let Him *roar* like the Lion of Judah.

As you recognize that it is Him and not you who is at work, you will come to understand the *jealousy of God* and *the fear of the Lord*. Hang on to your appreciation for the way He will not share His glory with another. Don't leave home without it!

The Holy Spirit does not always need you. Avoid the messiah complex that makes everything center around you. *Step out of the way* and let Him move in His own unique manner. Realize that He has His own specific timing and strategies, what we often call God's *kairos* timing. He does not expect you to know everything, so you do not need to act as if you do.

To walk in increased anointing, you will definitely need *patience*. This is the virtue that none of us wants but all of us need. You will also need a supernatural supply of *compassion,* which characterizes everything God does. Ask Him for more of His heart toward the people around you. Ask for more of His mercy, brokenness and humility. As you receive more of His heart, you will also receive a greater measure of His anointing.

When necessary, stop and *admit failure,* for that is the largest part of humility. Be willing to humble yourself, re-trace your steps and pick up where He left off. Make it a habit to *listen* for the still, small voice of the Spirit. The more you practice, the more of a habit it will become and the better you will hear. You are, after all, only taking *dancing lessons* with God. As you practice, you will learn to give in to the gentle nudges of the Holy Spirit, and that will be how His anointing will increase in your life and your ministry.

Time for Recess!

Recently, I heard the Holy Spirit say that classes were being offered in His "School of the Spirit"—but that it was time for recess. "Recess?" I responded. "What does recess mean?"

He replied, "It is time for activity to take place outside the walls. It is time for P. E.—Prophetic Evangelism." In the Spirit's timetable, it is time for supernatural activity to spill outside the walls of the Church and into the playgrounds, schools, streets, malls, and coffee shops where ordinary believers like you can be anointed vessels from which the presence and power of the Holy Spirit can spill out. The time of harvest is upon us. It's time to head for the fields, where the people are!

Those who are living truly supernatural life will be ready to step out. They will not know which way the wind is going to blow them, but they will be ready to hoist their sails and catch it. They will be the ones who, like Martha, go and fetch the Lord so that Mary and the others could sit at His feet.

To change the analogy, those who are living a supernatural life will be the ones who bring their empty vessels to be filled, as in the story of Elisha and the widow and the jar of oil (see 2 Kings 4). When you hear God calling you to step out in new ways, but you think that you are about to run out of anointing oil, remember the lessons of this story. Stop hoping for the Big Download to occur and ask Him how to increase your capacity as you pour out what you have. Here's how:

- *Go find empty vessels.* (Hint: They will be located outside your comfort zone. You must go outside of your own house to find them.) You will need more containers because you will need a greater capability to hold all of the anointing oil that He wants to multiply on you.

- *Bring your empty vessels into your secret place with God.* Bring to Him the needs that you have "borrowed."

- *Using what you have already, pour it out.* Give away what you have received up to this time. Do not hoard it or worry about it. Pour it out until there is no place left to pour it. Pour into the lives of others.

Do not waste time waiting for the next big encounter with God. Be faithful with the little you have and He will increase it. You will be naturally supernatural, able to move in the anointing of the Spirit wherever He may take you.

Review

You can stir yourself to greater faith and to a resulting greater anointing of the Holy Spirit. It is only by the anointing of the Spirit that you can live a truly supernatural life, a life that reflects God to the people around you because it includes radical demonstrations of His power infused with His loving compassion.

1. Can you describe the anointing of the Holy Spirit? What has been your experience of it?

2. Name several practical ways you can increase the anointing of the Spirit in your life.

3. In your own life, how have you seen God using you? Do you see a pattern? What are some personal lessons He has taught you?

Part III
Enforcing the Victory of Calvary

The ultimate key to your participation in the supernatural life is understanding what Jesus Christ accomplished through His life and ministry, His death, burial and resurrection—and what all of this means for you.

On the cross, Jesus opened the way to an eternal and supernatural life. How can you step through that open doorway? What does it mean to start living supernaturally and eternally, today?

On the cross, what did Jesus do to Satan? How does that protect you as you walk into a life of the Spirit, a supernatural way of life that inevitably will put you into more direct conflict with unseen evil than you used to have?

Are you somewhat afraid of what the devil might do to you? What can he do to you? What can he *not* do to you? Sometimes life is so difficult. Setbacks and defeats make us think that we must be going backward instead of forward. Too often we fail to reckon with the truth of the devil's dethronement and the hard-won (and permanent) *enthronement* of Jesus Christ in the heavenly realm, and we fail to understand the impact that such a major spiritual transaction has on our earthly realm.

Understanding all of these things is so important to your learning how to sail with the wind of the Spirit of

God. In this next section, we will review and explore: (1) the victorious power of the cross and the power of the blood of Christ; (2) the gifts and graces that have been bestowed on us through the cross; and (3) the victorious power of the unseen heavenly realm.

I want you to be fully equipped to be at home in the supernatural life!

Chapter 7

The Power of the Cross

"It is finished."

Jesus, nailed to a bloody wooden cross between two thieves, uttered those three final words and then slumped in death (see John 19:30).

From that moment on, nothing would ever be the same in the supernatural realm—nor would it ever be the same in the physical realm that you and I now inhabit more than 2,000 years later. Before that moment, the fallen angel we call Satan had been free to work his malicious will against anything and anybody in God's creation. But as soon as the Son of God expired on that rugged cross, the rules were changed.

Suddenly the barrier between heaven and earth was no longer impassible. Not long before He said, "It is finished," Jesus had told the repentant thief, "today you will be with me in paradise" (Luke 23:43). As soon as He completed the agony of dying, He opened the way to paradise. The enormous veil in the Temple that had kept the Holy of Holies sacrosanct was ripped from top to bottom, signifying that from that moment forward, it would be possible for anyone who stepped into Jesus' arms by faith to walk right into the holiest realm of heaven (see Luke 23:45). Furthermore, what transpired on that cross would allow believers, with whom you and I number ourselves, to begin to live heavenly life right here on earth. The Kingdom had come indeed.

Breaking the Chains

Without the cross, none of us would be talking about how to live the supernatural life. We would be lost—if we had managed to survive this long.

One of the primary facts about the cross is contained in John's brief statement: "The reason the Son of God appeared was to destroy the devil's work" (1 John 3:8). Greek lexicons unpack the word "destroy" with the following definitions: "(1) to loose any person (or thing) tied or fastened; . . . (2) to loose one bound, i.e. to unbind, release from bonds, set free . . . [one] bound with chains (a prisoner); . . . (3) to annul [laws], subvert . . . to do away with, to deprive of authority, whether by precept or act."[1] The word carries with it the sense of unbinding or unraveling.

I really like the concept of Jesus coming to destroy the works of the devil by *unraveling* them. It makes me think of a fly caught in a spider's web and that the cross can unravel the web of the enemy. We would be helpless without the power of the cross. Because of the cross, not only do we become empowered with divine intelligence as to what the devil's strategies are, but we also get to unravel them. We get to move in new kinds of strategic thinking with the renewed minds that God gives us as a part of the supernatural lifestyle into which we have been initiated.

Because of the cross, we are not limited to merely rebuking the enemy, although that is a valid thing to do with cross-bought authority. Because of the cross, we can *undo* the enemy's bindings. We can render them useless. We obtain revelations from God so that we can comprehend the enemy's schemes and then know how to pick them apart.

What kinds of schemes? What is the "devil's work"?

Morally, Satan entices people to sin. Physically, he inflicts disease. Intellectually, he seduces people and leads them into error. Spiritually, he binds the minds of unbelievers lest they see and believe the gospel.

We are familiar with the results of these kinds of schemes. We ourselves have been ensnared by them. The enemy of our souls continues to work evil in the world. The big difference, ever since the cross, is that the people who bear the name of Jesus can carry on Jesus' work of destroying the works of the devil. That is an absolutely supernatural job.

How Did Jesus Destroy the Works of the Devil?

During his years in Israel, Jesus met the enemy at every turn. The most obvious encounter occurred during his temptation in the desert (see Matt. 4:1-11), where He countered every challenge with "it is written," and quoted the truth from the written Word of God.

In another instance, recorded in Matthew 12, He delivered a blind and mute man who had been blind and mute because he was demon-possessed (see Matt. 12:22-29). The Pharisees accused Him of casting out the evil spirits by the power of Satan, but Jesus pointed out that if that were the case, it would mean that Satan's kingdom was divided against itself, and that the only way to execute effective deliverance was to come at the devil from the outside, bind the "strong man" first, and then take back whatever the strong man Satan had stolen and claimed as his own (see Luke 11:21-22). A large part of what Satan has captured is human souls. But now, with the coming of the Kingdom, the strong man could be bound and the captives set free.

A large part (one-quarter to one-third) of Jesus' earthly ministry consisted of deliverance. That should underline for us His statement that He came to destroy the works of the devil. He did it through His life and ministry, and He does it to this day through His holy guerrilla bands of disciples.

Following in the footsteps of Jesus, not only can believers destroy the works of the devil by rebuking him and sending him away, but they can also render devilish tactics useless. For instance, because (I assume) Satan and his demons are a restless and contentious bunch, it doesn't seem to take much for God's people, as strategic foot soldiers who come in to discern the enemy's weak spots, to speak confusion into his ranks so that the enemy forces develop internal strife and eventually self-destruct.

Jesus' Death

Jesus went about destroying the works of the devil before His crucifixion, and He is still destroying the works of the devil through the power of His death on the cross.

Satan's primary goal is to thwart the Father's goal of glorifying the Son. His secondary goal is to keep men and women in their sin, under its penalty, in bondage to its power, suffering mental and emotional defeat from its guilt-inducing accusations.

Jesus' death snatched Satan's goals away. When Jesus died as God's judgment against sin, His death undid the bonds of sin that had so demeaned God's glory. Thus, Satan's principal goal was thwarted. And when Jesus showed His disciples the way of faith in Him as their substitutionary sacrifice, Satan's secondary goal was thwarted. Henceforth, men and women of faith could bypass Satan's bondage, or if they had fallen into it, they could shake it off.

The cross gives glory to the Father and it vindicates the unworthy and the unrighteous—that's you and me— who accept by grace through faith the work of the cross. We sinners, who could never have been made right with God on our own, have been made righteous and perfect in God's eyes. That in itself glorifies God; and true to God's original goal, it glorifies Jesus. And then what happens is that the formerly unrighteous men and women who have been newly clothed in the righteousness of their Savior become sold-out worshipers of God. They in turn become empowered by the same Spirit that raised Christ Jesus from the dead. They now can both glorify God and become instruments of deliverance for their fellows.

Jesus' Resurrection and Exaltation

Of course, part of Satan's secondary goal is to keep believers from being successful. By his accusations, Satan persuades people that he still has the full power of death over them. He instills fear of death into the hearts of people and stirs up all sorts of mental and emotional defeat. Believers suffer almost as if they were unbelievers scraping their way through life, somehow enduring until the end.

That's where the power of the supernatural life should come in. What better way to defeat defeatism than with the abundantly supernatural, endlessly hope-filled life of the Holy Spirit? What better way to defeat death than by raising the dead back to life (see Heb. 2:14-15 and 1 Cor. 15:50-57)?

The resurrection was the Father's "Amen!" to the Son's "It is finished!" By raising Jesus from the dead and exalting Him to the right hand of the majesty on high, God the Father ratified, confirmed and openly proclaimed the all-sufficient power of the cross. His triumph was complete, forever (see Rom. 5:8-11; 1 Cor. 15:16-17; Eph. 1:18-23). King Jesus had absconded to heaven with the keys of death and Hades (see Rev. 1:17-18).

Closer to Heaven

In the account of what happened on that day of crucifixion, we read that the veil between the Holy of Holies and the rest of the Temple was torn in two (see Matt. 27:51; Mark 15:38; Luke 23:45). As I noted above, this is a perfect symbol for what has happened to the invisible but very effective dividing "curtain" between the earthly realm and the heavenly realm. Now that Jesus Christ has been crucified, the heavy veil that was like a divider made of drapery has become a set of curtains that you can push aside and walk through. Ordinary believers can do it. Once they are on the inside of the supernatural, they can enjoy great freedom to explore.

For some time now, I have been collecting and reading books about eternity. The idea to start doing this probably came from the Holy Spirit. Eventually, I expect to teach and write about it. But for now, I'm still collecting, praying, pondering and musing.

Right in the middle of my collecting books about heaven and hell, my wife graduated to become a resident of heaven. Now she is on the other side of that veil, permanently. As a result, for me the veil between the temporal and the eternal has become enormously thin. In an all-new way, I'm walking in the supernatural life. The grief and pain are still with me, but so is the victory of the cross. The sting of death has been removed; it really has. I still miss my dear wife. But I will be united with her again one day! All because of the work of the cross of Jesus Christ!

The cross makes it possible for you and me to set our feet on the path to heaven and stay the course with joy. The cross makes it possible for us to develop the godly character we need in order to become holy vessels for the Holy Spirit. The cross makes it possible for us to walk the supernatural highway all the way to the Father's house, where Jesus said there are many "mansions" or individual dwelling places for those of us who believe in Him (see John 14:2). Jesus told His disciples, "If I go and prepare a place for you, I will come back and take you to be with me that you also may be where I am" (John 14:3).

Where did Jesus come from? He came from the bosom of His Father. Where did He go back to? To the bosom of His Father. What is the "bosom of the Father"? The heart of God Himself. That's where Jesus is preparing a place for each one of us, so that we can be with Him. Our destination isn't some vast, impersonal heaven; it is the very heart of God Himself.

And—here we are again—we get appetizers served up to us on this side. As we explore this idea of living supernaturally, we get to taste and have our taste buds whetted concerning the Father's heaven-heart. We have a goal, and even though the journey may seem long to us, our supernatural walk comes with refreshments.

The Blood of Christ Avails

The old-fashioned word "avails" means "serves to bring you gain." The blood of Jesus, shed on the cross, brings abundant benefits to those who "avail themselves" of it.

Scripture tells us about the many benefits of Jesus' blood that was shed on the cross. According to Hebrews 12:24, Jesus has established a new covenant through His blood, and He is interceding on our behalf to establish this blood covenant with each of us. As we agree with and testify about what Jesus' blood has accomplished, we take hold of those benefits, simultaneously overcoming the evil of the enemy. Revelation 12:11 states, "They overcame him [the accuser of the brethren] by the blood of the Lamb and by the word of their testimony."

There are at least seven distinct ways that the blood of Jesus avails for us. As we consider them, proclaim them, testify about them and pray through them, we will find that we will be walking in a fuller supernatural life. The accuser has to back off in the face of such testimony. What else can he do?

1. *Forgiveness.* We have been forgiven through the blood of Jesus. "The law requires that nearly everything be cleansed with blood, and without the shedding of blood there is no forgiveness" (Heb. 9:22). Satan cannot succeed when he tries to tell us that our sins will bring us down, because we know otherwise.

2. *Cleansing.* The blood of Jesus has cleansed us from all sin (see 1 John 1:7; 1 Pet. 1:2). Not only are we forgiven, but also the stains of sin have been washed away. We have been freed from condemnation and shame. We have been cleansed from remorse and regret. In addition, we have been cleansed from dead works to which we used to resort in our efforts to become godly.

3. *Redemption.* We have been redeemed by the blood of the Lamb (see Eph. 1:7; 1 Pet. 1:18-19). That means our freedom has been purchased with the cost of that sacrificial blood, so that we could be transferred over from the kingdom of darkness to the kingdom of light.

4. *Justification.* Being justified by Jesus' blood means that it is just as if we had never sinned, which means that we are righteous in His sight. "God made him who had no sin to be sin for us, so that in him we might become the righteousness of God" (2 Cor. 5:21). Now we do not need to suffer punishment for our

sins, which would have been the automatic result when our unrighteousness encountered God's perfect righteousness (see Rom. 5:9).

5. *Sanctification.* Not only have we been forgiven and cleansed and redeemed and justified, but we have also been sanctified, which means that we have been set apart. We have been pulled out of Satan's territory and set apart for God's good purposes (see Heb. 13:12).

6. *Peace.* "God purposed that through (by the service, the intervention of) Him [the Son] all things should be completely reconciled back to Himself, whether on earth or in heaven, as through Him, [the Father] made peace by means of the blood of His cross" (Col. 1:20, *AMP*).

7. *Access.* Because of Jesus' blood shed on the cross, we now have full confidence to enter the Most Holy Place. The veil has been torn in two. Access has been granted. (See Heb. 10:19; Eph. 2:13-14.)

If you really have accepted the completed work of the cross of Jesus, which means that you believe that it is effective and that what it accomplished is permanent, your internal war is over. You have the kingdom of God within you—righteousness, peace and joy in the Holy Spirit (see Rom. 14:17). You have access to God directly. You have confidence to enter the most holy place.

That, my friend, is supernatural life!

The Blood that Speaks

Let's take a quick glimpse of one of the most inspiring pictures of life on the other side that you'll ever find. It's a peek inside the veil:

> But you have come to Mount Zion, to the heavenly Jerusalem, the city of the living God. You have come to thousands upon thousands of angels in joyful assembly, to the church of the firstborn, whose names are written in heaven. You have come to God, the judge of all men, to the spirits of righteous men made perfect, to Jesus the mediator of a new covenant, and to the sprinkled blood that speaks a better word than the blood of Abel (Heb. 12:22-24).

Here we find, first of all, a description of God's dwelling place. Second, we see a picture of those who dwell there with God. Last but not least, we are given a glimpse of God Himself, God the Judge of all, Jesus our Mediator and the precious blood that "speaks."

Now, what does that mean? It is far beyond our everyday experience. We can find a precedent, however, if we look back at the book of Genesis. In the fourth chapter, we find the unhappy account of the rivalry between Cain and Abel. Cain became jealous and angry of his brother, and he yielded to the sinful impulses within him. When the two of them were alone together in a field, Cain rose up and killed his younger brother, Abel.

Then God asked Cain where his brother was, and Cain answered rudely, "How should I know? Am I my brother's keeper?" (see Gen. 4:9). Whereupon the Lord said, "What have you done? Listen! Your brother's blood cries out to me from the ground" (Gen. 4:10).

This is an illustration of the principle that runs throughout the Scriptures: "life is in the blood" (see Lev. 17:11). Not only is there life in the blood, but innocent blood seems to have particular attributes when it is spilled. It cries out for reparation. But, we are told in the passage from Hebrews above, before the presence of our Judge in heaven, Jesus' blood speaks better than the blood of Abel or any of his implicit offspring. That blood cries out for mercy, and mercy triumphs over judgment (see Jas. 2:13).

The innocent blood of Jesus is a continuous reminder before our Father of the sacrifice of His precious Son. The blood of Jesus is the greatest and most effective plea before God, the devil and the world.

There is, therefore, no more prevailing argument that we can bring before the throne of God than that of the sufferings and death of His Son. By ourselves, we have no merit at all. We cannot prevail because of our prayer techniques or by virtue of some special past experience. Because of Jesus' shed blood and because of our faith, we can escape punishment and banishment, and we can bring others with us to the Father's heart.

Charles Spurgeon once said, "Many keys fit many locks, but the master key is the blood and the name of Him that died and rose again, and ever lives in heaven to save unto the uttermost. The blood of Christ is that which unlocks the treasury of heaven."[2]

Plead the blood; surrender to the truth of its power and allow the Spirit of the One who died to cry out through you. Plead the power of the cross. Sing about the blood. Recite the Scriptures about it. Do your part to enforce the victory of Jesus over the powers of darkness.

Say it so that heaven and earth can hear: "Through the blood of Christ Jesus, I have been redeemed and cleansed and forgiven. Through His blood, I have been sanctified and made holy, and I am set apart to God. My body is a temple of the Holy Spirit. Satan has no place in me, no claim over me, no power over me—because of the blood that Jesus shed for me and for many."

Agree with His triumphant cry, "It is finished!" Jesus has overcome the devil and He has opened the way to heaven once and for all, accomplishing it in one death-defying sacrifice so that each and every one of us could be ushered into the place He has prepared for us.

Review

The only reason any of us has access to a supernatural life with God is because of what His Son did on the cross. Without that ultimate sacrifice, the way to heaven would have remained barricaded, because none of us could have come into the presence of God; we were too sin-saturated and we had been captured by Satan, the enemy of God.

By acknowledging the power of the cross and the power of the blood that was shed there, we can defeat the devil and freely step into the Kingdom.

1. Why do we say that the resurrection was the Father's "amen" to the Son's "it is finished"?

2. Choose at least two of the powerful benefits of the cross and expand upon them from your own experience. You will be giving glory to God as you do so, and you will be driving the devil farther away.

3. When did you step through that veil that was torn in two by the power of Jesus' death? How has your life since that time been a supernatural one?

Chapter 8

Tools for Your Tool Belt

The Holy Spirit is ambidextrous. He is the original multitasker. He can do far more than one thing at a time, and He always does everything well.

With the Holy Spirit living inside you, you become part of His activity in the world. He captures your attention so that He can direct your participation. He equips you with tools because His work requires more than your "bare hands" of human strength and ability. He motivates you, He energizes you, and He rewards you. Like a master contractor, He is perfectly capable of doing every aspect of a job Himself, but He distributes aspects of the job to you and others, helping you all to work together well.

You must have supernatural tools in order to live a supernatural life in the Spirit (although some of what the Spirit considers tools may surprise you). The more you can learn about using the tools in your Holy Spirit tool belt, the better you will be able to tackle the situations He brings you into and the better you will be able to help usher in His kingdom.

The Power Tool of Faith

Faith is a major power tool that you absolutely must have with your equipment. The power tool of faith will help you move mountains of opposition and it will help you create new structures based on supernatural blueprints.

The overall importance of the power tool of faith can be seen in this line from the letter to the Hebrews: "without faith it is impossible to please God, because anyone who comes to him must believe that he exists and that he rewards those who earnestly seek him" (Heb. 11:6).

Your faith, once it gets plugged into God, connects you to Him. Your faith gives you the ability to believe what He says in His Word and to appropriate it in your life. Faith is a constant, abiding trust toward God (not toward your feelings or toward your circumstances or toward other people). Faith is a matter of your heart and spirit, not your head. You put your faith in God because of who He is, not because you are so smart yourself. Your faith is not in yourself at all.

God is a rewarder of those who seek Him with faith because of who He is. His Word is as true as He is trustworthy. God cannot lie. When you put your whole trust in Him, you will not be disappointed.

True faith is in the present tense, which distinguishes it from future-oriented hope. You need present-tense faith in order to have your future-tense hopes fulfilled. That's what it says in the well-known passage from Hebrews, here in four versions so you can better see what I mean:

Faith is the substance of things hoped for, the evidence of things not seen (Heb. 11:1, *KJV*).

Faith is being sure of what we hope for and certain of what we do not see (Heb. 11:1).

Faith is the assurance of things hoped for, the conviction of things not seen (Heb. 11:1, *NASB*).

Faith is the assurance (the confirmation, the title deed) of the things [we] hope for, being the proof of things [we] do not see and the conviction of their reality [faith perceiving as real fact what is not revealed to the senses] (Heb. 11:1, *AMP*).

The Greek word that is translated "faith" here—and numerous other times in the New Testament—is the noun *pistis*. The word refers to reliability, faithfulness, that which causes trust. It can also mean a solemn promise, an oath, a proof or a pledge. In the active sense, it simply means confidence or trust.[1] When you put your trust and faith in something you "believe," the verb in Greek is *pisteuo*. When you believe in something, you are convinced that it is true. When you trust and believe in God, not only are you convinced that He is reliable, but you are also convinced that He is willing and able to help you.[2]

Believing faith, according to this passage from Hebrews, is a *present reality*, as opposed to being merely optimistic. Your faith is not the same as your hoped-for and much-desired objective—your faith is the means of obtaining it.

Faith is the "title deed" to the promises of God. It is the "assurance" of things that are out of sight. If you tell me that you own a piece of property in another state, how do I know that is the truth? Your proof, or assurance, cannot be just "a lot of blab and go grab"; your proof is your title deed. If you can produce the deed, then there is no question about it; you own that piece of property. Your title deed is your legal evidence of ownership, and it cannot be contested. Faith proves the truth of God's promises and provision.

How Does Faith Differ from Hope?

Hope, as I said, has to do with the future, whereas faith has to do with the *present*. Hope is not a present reality as faith is. Hope, rather, is an expectation or a desire for the future. Hope has to do with waiting, while faith has to do with *how* you wait: "we through the Spirit, by faith, are waiting for the hope of righteousness" (Gal. 5:5, *NASB*).

In his teaching, "The Helmet of Hope," Derek Prince defined hope as the "confident expectation of good, a steady and persistent optimism." To be a pessimist is to deny your faith, for "we know that in all things God works for the good of those who love him, who have been called according to his purpose" (Rom. 8:28).

So you have to understand what hope is before you can ever operate in faith. Hope is like a helmet. In fact, Scripture urges us to put on "faith and love as a breast-plate, and the hope of salvation as a helmet" (1 Thess. 5:8). You put hope on your head—on your mind. And it is interesting to note that a Roman military helmet fit over the front of the head (like putting hope on your mind) and it also had flaps that went over the ears. Through our helmets of hope, we have to filter what we think and hear. Then our hearts can reach up into the "substance of things hoped for" and make faith out of it.

After waiting in hope a long time, you get to a kind of tipping point. Some kind of transaction happens. You have hoped long enough. At last your heart grabs hold of the things hoped for and you have *assurance*. You may not need to pray anymore. You are so sure, you can start praising God for the yet-unseen results of your prayers.

Without Christ we can have no such hope (see Eph. 2:12; 1 Thess. 4:13), for hope is rooted in saving faith (see Rom. 5:1-5). Both faith and hope deal with the realm of things unseen (see Rom. 8:24; 2 Cor. 5:7) and both are founded upon God's Word (see Rom. 10:17).

Faith—Seeing into the Realm of the Unseen

Faith sees into the realm of the unseen and calls it forth as a present reality. Faith makes it possible for us to live our lives supernaturally. "We live by faith, not by sight" (2 Cor. 5:7). We can see how living by faith is contrasted with living by sight in scriptural passages such as the following:

> We fix our eyes not on what is seen, but on what
> is unseen. For what is seen is temporary, but what
> is unseen is eternal (2 Cor. 4:18).

> I am still confident of this:
> I will see the goodness of the Lord
> in the land of the living (Ps. 27:13).

> Jesus said, "Did I not tell you that if you believed,
> you would see the glory of God?" (John 11:40).

Faith is a *certainty*. How can we have such certainty? Our certainty of faith comes from the certainty of the Word of God. "Faith comes from hearing the message, and the message is heard through the word of Christ" (Rom. 10:17). Nothing is more certain than the Word of God (see Num. 23:19; Ps. 89:30-31; Isa. 55:11; Rom. 4:20-21)!

Now I need to get real here. You need to know that the certainty of faith does *not* mean that God will tell you everything. In fact, in your supernatural life with Him, He will make sure that you do *not* know everything that is taking place. You may be very "prophetic," but that does not mean that you will know everything. Take it from me, God will show you only enough to go on. The rest you will have to fill in by faith. It is as if He skips a stone across a big pond and it touches down on A, B and C, skips D, E, F and G, touches down on H, I and J, hops over L, M, N, O and P, hits Q, R, S and then—*whoosh*—you get to Z. For those in-between steps, you're relying on faith. God leaves those blanks in there. He does not want you to walk by sight. He wants you to walk by your obedient faith.

He does not have to tell me to get up out of bed in the morning. He doesn't have to remind me to brush my teeth. He should not have to tell me to read my Bible and pray. He expects me to follow the basic principles of His kingdom, and He expects me to use my own understanding, acknowledging Him and being ready to move with Him.

Your faith is not a certainty because it makes you omniscient. Your faith is a certainty because of the omniscient, omnipotent, omnipresent One you believe in.

Faith Must Involve Action

Faith is pointless and useless unless it accomplishes something. That is what the apostle James tells us:

Faith by itself, if it does not have works, is dead. But someone will say, "You have faith, and I have works." Show me your faith without your works, and I will show you my faith by my works (Jas. 2:17-18, *NKJV*).

As we receive faith from God's truth, we learn to put our trust in what He says. We learn to believe, pray and even command our circumstances to align themselves with His truth.

Motivated by God's command and his trust in Him, Noah went against the prevailing circumstances and built the ark (see Heb. 11:7). He could have just waited for clearer indications. Sure, God spoke and said it was going to rain, but it hadn't rained in a long, long time; in fact, it had never rained. Arks cost money. It's silly to build a big boat on dry land if you don't have anywhere to launch it. People who do things like that look like fools.

Noah could have taken a passive position in his faith. He could have thought, *Somebody ought to do something. I'm just waiting on God.* Instead, he acted. He was obedient. His faith had legs—and his toolbox was useful too. Like you and me, he had to take each step by faith, because he really did not know how to build an ark. As he did something with each word he heard, God would give him the next word. First it was, "Build me an ark."

"What should I build it out of?"

"Gopher or cypress wood."

"Plain wood won't work. It's not waterproof. How do I waterproof it?"

"Tar and pitch."

And so Noah proceeded, step by step by step—working by faith (see Gen. 6:14).

With Your Measure of Faith

Paul's letter to the Romans says that we each have received a measure of faith, and that our faith has to do with our confidence (see Rom. 12:3). But we have to use it or lose it. Like a man who goes to the gym to work out, we have to build our faith-muscles by actually lifting things with them. You have basic musculature. How are you building those muscles up? What action steps are you taking?

Faith must have an action or an expression. Your circumstances will defy God's expressed will. They won't line up. Your emotions and your logic may not line up either. You may have to have a word with them. You may have to speak to them to make them line up. Like Ezekiel, you may have to command some "dry bones" to stand up and live (see Ezek. 37).

Your life will be full of dry bones and broken, fragmented structures. It may have been that way as long as you can remember. God says, "Speak to them." Tell them to come into alignment with His will. That is what Peter did when the man who had been lame from birth begged alms from him. The man had a measure of faith (although he expected to receive only money, not healing) and Peter did too. Peter's faith was big enough for complete healing. Peter, who did not have any money anyway, gave the beggar a lot more than he was asking for. Peter commanded his useless feet to operate as if they had never been lame:

Peter looked straight at him, as did John. Then Peter said, "Look at us!" So the man gave them his attention, expecting to get something from them.

Then Peter said, "Silver or gold I do not have, but what I have I give you. In the name of Jesus Christ of Nazareth, walk." Taking him by the right hand, he helped him up, and instantly the man's feet and ankles became strong. He jumped to his feet and began to walk. Then he went with them into the temple courts, walking and jumping, and praising God (Acts 3:4-8).

Peter is a great example of someone who is living a supernatural life, which is a life of faith-based action, one that is ready for the next gust of wind from the Spirit.

You already have a measure of faith. What you do with it is up to you. It is not God's responsibility to make you exercise it, although His Spirit will help you. In the supernatural life you will face all kinds of uncertain circumstances, and you will have to use your measure of faith; as you do so, your faith will increase (see Luke 17:5-6). At times you will have an increased anointing or a gift of faith. That's when you can speak to the circumstances.

Speak to the sun. Speak to the wind. Speak to the bones. Speak to the sickness. Command them to line up with the Word of God. Do something with the measure of faith you have. Live a supernatural life of faith-based action!

Prayer: A Tool for Every Tool Belt

Every believer in Christ Jesus has a birthright; they can approach the throne of grace to obtain health and mercy in time of need. Prayer—communing and conversing with God—is like the key to the storehouse. It is the tool of access. And it is on *every* believer's tool belt, like an equal opportunity access card. Just call out "Help!" (which is a prayer) and watch what happens.

Prayer Is Ministry at the Altar of Incense

Prayer is like the ministry at the altar of incense, where only priests could go, because in Christ Jesus, we are all priests. Like Zechariah, when it was his turn to minister at the altar of incense, our experience can be supernatural because of one thing: what goes up must also come down.

Zechariah arrived to pray and minister to the Lord at the "hour of incense," and the people were all in prayer outside (see Luke 1). What went up (incense = prayer) came back down to earth in the form of an angelic visitation. The angel Gabriel proclaimed that the barrenness of his wife, Elizabeth, would be healed and that a son would be born to them, a son they should name "John." Zechariah went back home, his wife became pregnant and their son, John the Baptist, was born nine months later.

Praying Down the Supernatural

Zechariah, a man of God who was simply acting according to his duties, ended up praying down the supernatural miracle that occurred.

I am convinced that in our own day we are crossing the threshold in the Spirit into a new, supernatural place of miracles. Among other evidences, I have noticed that in more than one place at the same time, but without prior knowledge of each other, people have completed

40-day fasts, praying specifically for a miraculous out-pouring. One was in Texas (Mike and Cindy Jacobs, Generals International). They were re-digging the wells of the Healing Voice, a ministry connected with Gordon Lindsay's Christ for the Nations. Another was in Arizona (Patricia King, Extreme Prophetic). They were contending in the Spirit for supernatural miracles to be released in Phoenix, which has had a history of supernatural miracles and which is where A. A. Allen had his Miracle Valley.

While I was in Jerusalem on the Day of Atonement, on a recent prayer tour, I received a detailed dream that depicted increased authority over demonic realms and outbreaks of miraculous supernatural activity. Jesus is the one who said, "If two of you on earth agree about anything you ask for, it will be done for you by my Father in heaven" (Matt. 18:19). It appears to me as if the Holy Spirit is stirring up faith and prayer in the Body of Christ across the world, and that miracles are on the way.

Join your prayers with others. Pray that God will come and perform in our day the miracles we read about in the Bible, such as healing the deaf, dumb and blind; delivering those who are oppressed by demons; healing those with mental problems; raising the dead; healing those who cannot walk; nourishing those who have no food; Jesus Himself visiting the unsaved and telling them how to be saved.

If you are in touch with Christian news reports, you know about some current miracles along these lines, including resurrections of the dead. The supernatural realm is breaking into the natural realm, and it is happening because so many believers have taken prayer off their tool belts and they have used it in concert with others.

Spiritual Gifts: Special Tools for Special Situations

Besides the power tool of faith and the power tool of prayer that every believer has on his or her spiritual tool belt, we all carry other, more specialized tools. These are called spiritual gifts. Gifts cannot be earned; they are simply given to us. They are presents to us from our loving Father. Our job is to receive them and learn to use them for the glory of God.

Here is my list of 25 of these spiritual gifts, in alphabetical order. Which ones have you found on your supernatural tool belt?

1. Gifts of *administration* or governing (see 1 Cor. 12:28)
2. The gift of *apostle* (see 1 Cor. 12:28; Eph. 4:11)
3. The gift of *celibacy* (see 1 Cor. 7:7)
4. The gift of *discerning of spirits* (see 1 Cor. 12:10)
5. The gift of *eternal life* (see Rom. 6:23)
6. The gift of being an *evangelist* (see Eph. 4:11)
7. The gift of *exhortation* (encouragement; see Rom. 12:8)
8. The gift of *faith* (see 1 Cor. 12:9)
9. The gift of liberal *giving* (see Rom. 12:8)
10. Gifts of *healings* (see 1 Cor. 12:9)
11. Gifts of *helps* (those who help others; see 1 Cor. 12:28)
12. The gift of the *interpretation of tongues* (see 1 Cor. 12:10)
13. The gift of *leadership* (governing, ruling; see Rom. 12:8)

14. The gift of showing *mercy* (doing acts of mercy; see Rom. 12:8)
15. The gift of *miraculous powers* (the working of miracles; see 1 Cor. 12:10)
16. The gift of *pastor* (shepherd; see Eph. 4:11)
17. The gift of *prophecy* (see 1 Cor. 12:10)
18. The office of *prophet* (see 1 Cor. 12:28; Eph. 4:11)
19. The gift of *righteousness* (see Rom. 5:17)
20. The gift of *service* (serving; see Rom. 12:7)
21. The office of *teacher* (see 1 Cor. 12:28; Eph. 4:11)
22. The gift of *teaching* (see Rom. 12:7)
23. The gift of speaking in different kinds of *tongues* (see 1 Cor. 12:10)
24. The gift of the *word of knowledge* (see 1 Cor. 12:8)
25. The gift of the *word of wisdom* (see 1 Cor. 12:8)

Some people would add the gift of *martyrdom*, but the Bible does not specify that as a gift. (I think it's a destination!) You will note that some gifts, such as prophecy and teaching, also can come in a more powerful and consistent form, and we call that an "office." You will also note that I included more gifts than many others do in lists of spiritual gifts. It seems to me that the scriptural gifts of *life* and *righteousness* are just as prominent on our spiritual tool belts as faith and prayer.

Other possible spiritual gifts that you might find on your spiritual tool belt include the following:

- craftsmanship
- encouragements
- fastings

- hospitality
- intercessory prayer
- interpretation of dreams
- being a judge
- being a missionary or doing cross-cultural ministry
- music
- philanthropy
- being a worship leader

(As you may have realized, worship and prayer cannot be found in scriptural gift lists. They are nowhere listed as special gifts of the Holy Spirit. Either this means that they are "everyone" gifts, like faith, or they are special "unlisted" gifts. We have to pull together gift lists from quite a few different places in Scripture, and no one list is authoritative.)

You, along with any believer, can expect to find that God has gifted you with more than one of these tools on your spiritual tool belt. Your set of tools may include revelatory gifts, "power" gifts or gifts that depend on your ability to recount the truth verbally. Your future may hold one or more ministries or offices of the Spirit. One thing is for sure: You will not have been missed in the distribution, because you belong to God.

Living by Faith

Faith is a lifestyle, a supernatural one. Living by faith is the only way to continue living in Christ day after day and year after year.

To live the supernatural life, everything you do must issue from your faith, even choosing which foods to eat. In fact, "everything that does not come from faith is sin" (Rom. 14:23). That does not mean that you need a word from on high for every action you take; but it does mean that your focus is on God for everything, big and small. If you have a problem or a question, He's the one you go to first. If you want direction, likewise. You recognize that He will sometimes provide for you through human means or your own hard work, but you will also realize that everything in your life comes from Him and circulates back to Him.

The person who lives by faith has unlimited potential (see Matt. 19:26; Mark 9:23). This potential does not give you liberty to do whatever you please, but instead to seek God's will and ways and then soar on the wind of His Spirit.

Supernatural Life Is Faith Working Through Love

God's unconditional acceptance of those who trust in His Son, combined with Paul's teaching about grace, could be misunderstood to mean that it does not really matter how you live. It is true that there is nothing you can do to earn His loving acceptance. In fact, if you try to earn it through religious rituals or rules and regulations, you will, in effect, spurn His salvation. He loves you. He has chosen to accept you into His kingdom. You have accepted His acceptance by surrendering to His Son, who died so that you would not have to pay the price of your sinfulness.

Far from being an excuse for further sinning, God's grace sets you free from the bondage of sin so that you can live a life of righteousness in obedience to God—i.e., a supernatural one. God's grace enables you to work out your salvation as God's Spirit works within you, making your desires match His and giving you the ability to perform His will (see Phil. 2:12-13). God gives you sufficient grace for every good work (see 2 Cor. 9:8). The Lord strengthens you (see 2 Thess. 2:16-17) and equips you (see Heb. 13:20-21) for every good work.

> For the grace of God that brings salvation has appeared to all men. It teaches us to say "No" to ungodliness and worldly passions, and to live self-controlled, upright and godly lives in this present age, while we wait for the blessed hope— the glorious appearing of our great God and Savior, Jesus Christ, who gave himself for us to redeem us from all wickedness and to purify for himself a people that are his very own, eager to do what is good (Titus 2:11-14).

For your part, you need to express your faith in action. Although you were saved by grace through faith and not through your own works (see Eph. 2:8-9; Titus 3:5), your saving faith results in a supernaturally empowered lifestyle of good works (see Eph. 2:10; Titus 3:7-8).

Supernatural life is faith working through love. It is the love of God that keeps me going. It is the love of God that helps me to never quit. It is the love of God that causes me to believe in the reality of the supernatural life when I haven't seen it all manifested yet. Love is supernatural. Without God, who *is* love, anything we might think is love is a mere shadow of the real thing (see 1 John 4:8).

The love that has been poured out in our hearts by the Holy Spirit (see Rom. 5:5) overflows to fulfill the law (see Rom. 13:8-10). This love has both a vertical (God-ward) focus and a horizontal (humanward) focus.

Jesus summed up the whole of the Old Testament Scriptures with His two love commands: " 'Love the Lord your God with all your heart and with all your soul and with all your mind.' This is the first and greatest commandment. And the second is like it: 'Love your neighbor as yourself' " (Matt. 22:37-39). That is the essence of the supernatural life. Because of the Lord's love commands, Paul could say, "The only thing that counts is faith expressing itself through love" (Gal. 5:6).

Repent if You Need To

Now, if you find that you have fallen short of living by faith (and most of us have), there is no substitute for humble repentance. Some of us need to repent for our fears and prejudices against a "faith emphasis." We need to repent for being afraid of what a faith lifestyle might look like or what others have made it look like. Others of us need to repent for our fear of what living by faith could cost us.

Faith in Action

It is time to step into the Holy of Holies. It's time to pray and to act. Like Zechariah on the momentous day when it was his turn to minister at the altar of incense, let's believe God for supernatural encounters, healing and miracles.

Let's pull the tools from our spiritual tool belts that were provided for us for such a time as this. From faith working through love, we draw out mercy and wisdom and tongues and prophecy and administration and pastoring and evangelism and helps and miracles. It takes more than one good carpenter to build a good house. Let us, all together, become a part of the supernatural company that exercises faith in God and works to build up the Body of Christ on the earth. May God's kingdom come and may His will be done.

Review

You must have supernatural tools in order to live a supernatural life in the Spirit. Those tools range from basic ones with which everyone is provided, such as faith, love, life, righteousness and prayer, to very specific "specialty" tools such as gifts of healings or words of knowledge.

1. What are some of the spiritual gifts or tools that you have found on your own God-given tool belt?

2. How are you actively exercising your faith? Have you seen your faith grow stronger as a result?

3. How has living by faith engaged you in living the supernatural life?

Chapter 9

Help Is on the Way!

You and I live a supernatural life. One of the best parts of living a supernatural life is by the company we keep. The Holy Spirit and angels of all descriptions are as close as our next breath. Supernatural guidance and heavenly encounters are just around the next corner.

Thank the Lord that we have not been left alone to accomplish His purposes and plans. Thank Jesus for fulfilling His promise to send us another Helper, the Holy Spirit, to dwell in our hearts. Thank Him that when we call on Him, He answers. "Therefore let us draw near with confidence to the throne of grace, so that we may receive mercy and find grace to help in time of need" (Heb. 4:16, *NASB*).

Living the supernatural life, we have guaranteed access to the throne of grace, where we can find supernatural aid. Help from the throne of grace can take many forms. Let's explore some of them in this chapter.

Your Access to Divine Guidance

As you live the supernatural life, taking up your cross daily and walking in integrity and holiness—there are no shortcuts, remember—you need to cultivate the spirit of revelation. Paul prayed this prayer for the Ephesian believers, and we can pray it ourselves:

I keep asking that the God of our Lord Jesus Christ, the glorious Father, may give you the Spirit of wisdom and revelation, so that you may know him better. I pray also that the eyes of your heart may be enlightened in order that you may know the hope to which he has called you, the riches of his glorious inheritance in the saints, and his incomparably great power for us who believe. That power is like the working of his mighty strength (Eph. 1:17-19).

Having the Spirit of wisdom and revelation resident within you means that you can hear His voice. Will you always hear it and recognize it? No. Can you learn to hear it better? Yes, you can, even if you feel that you have rarely or never heard God's voice before.

In my other book in this series, *The Beginner's Guide to Hearing God,* I put forward the idea that the Holy Spirit within us helps us home in on God's guiding voice like a supernatural Geiger counter:

It's an interesting instrument [the Geiger counter], named for Hans Geiger, the German physicist who invented it in 1928. The Geiger counter can detect the presence and intensity of radiation (the spontaneous emission or energy from radioactive elements, most notably uranium) by using a gas-filled tube that briefly conducts electricity when radiation makes the gas conductive. The Geiger counter amplifies this signal into a series of clicks. The closer it gets to the radioactive substance and the greater the intensity of the sub-

stance's radiation, the louder and faster the clicking noise becomes.

I have often thought this is a lot like our approach to hearing God's voice. Our spirit is like
the Geiger counter that tells us whether we are
closer or father away. It helps us put all the pieces
together. We learn to pay attention to an inner
witness. We check in with the Holy Spirit, we listen to our "knower," and our spirit either bears
witness, or it doesn't. When we are filled with the
Holy Spirit, we have a divine guidance system
that comes as part of the package.[1]

Have you had the experience of "clicking" with the
still, small voice of God's Spirit? You can increase your
sensitivity to His voice by meeting His preconditions. If
you read Isaiah 58, you will find some of those preconditions. They include honoring God and caring for the
poor and downtrodden, refraining from accusation of
others and, above all, maintaining a humble heart.

Besides preparing your heart, you need to know that
hearing God's voice and determining God's guidance is
more of an art form than a set technique. Yet there are basic ground rules that you need to be aware of. They will
help you find God Himself, which is even better than
finding His will for your life. As you draw closer to Him,
You will walk in His will increasingly.

God Speaks Through His Written Word
I have put this one first for a reason—it's the most important principle of divine guidance. In order to be grounded

solidly in the Word and intimately familiar with it, you need to read it daily.

The number-one way that the Holy Spirit will speak to you will always involve reading your Bible, hearing good Bible-based preaching or having a good conversation about the Word. You will find that certain biblical phrases and concepts will just "come alive" at certain times, under the spotlight of His Spirit.

Now, whenever you think you are hearing a new word from God, you have something objective to hold it up against. All of your supernatural experiences need to line up with the written Word of God. Your sense about God's will for your life's direction needs to line up with it too.

I hope you know that you cannot take the "Bible roulette" route every time and expect to come up with an accurate measure of the veracity of what you think God is telling you. But when you think you are hearing God's voice, you can expect to find confirmation of His direction through a careful consideration of what you find in your Bible. It is an amazing Book, and you will find out a lot about how to live the supernatural life within its pages.

God Confirms His Will Through Circumstances

Circumstances alone do not constitute divine guidance, but they can certainly confirm God's will.

In *The Beginner's Guide to Hearing God*, I told the story of how I almost quit college because I was so excited about serving God and impatient about getting on with the rest of my life. Only six months before graduation, I almost quit. But before I did, I asked God to do something to show me His will. Suddenly I received notification that I had been awarded a scholarship for which I had not applied. It was a religious "leadership" scholarship, meant to help me financially at my secular university. I accepted it, and I completed my degree. That's a good example of a circumstantial confirmation of a decision.

God Speaks in Your Heart

We use the terms "heart" and "spirit" interchangeably. So when I say that God speaks in your heart or to your heart, your heart is the same as your spirit. He speaks to you, Spirit to spirit.

The Holy Spirit dwells in your heart, and He speaks from where He dwells. Have you listened to your heart lately? What is beating in your heart? As you learn and grow in your supernatural walk, the heartbeat of God's Spirit will be reflected in yours, increasingly.

"When he, the Spirit of truth, comes, he will guide you into all truth. He will not speak on his own; he will speak only what he hears, and he will tell you what is yet to come" (John 16:13).

Look for God's Peace

God speaks by peace as He gives peace to His listener. Again we see it in a psalm: "I will listen to what God the Lord will say; he promises peace to his people, his saints" (Ps. 85:8).

Conversely, if you feel pushed and unsettled, if you feel you're being rushed or under pressure, then you are not hearing the Holy Spirit. You may be hearing your own frantic feelings or someone else's strong ideas or even the words of the devil. But without peace, it is not God.

Now, it is true that you might need to work through some un-peaceful emotions before you can find His peace. The fact that you are looking for peace does not mean that there will be no storm or no conflict. Yet God's peace will provide a quiet haven in the midst of turbulence.

The peace of God is sure-footed and consistent. It does not change tactics or alter its assumptions. The peace of God indicates that the wisdom of God is in the room (see Jas. 3:17).

God's guidance can wait patiently and peacefully. It is not in a hurry. He Himself is never too late. His word can stand the test of time. God is not the author of confusion, but rather of peace (see 1 Cor. 14:33).

Expect the Unexpected

If you have trained your spiritual ears to listen for Him, God will often speak to you when you least expect it. He will say something to you when you first wake up from sleep. He will zing a thought into your head when you are driving your car or mowing the lawn.

He will also guide you so subtly that you are unaware of His nudges. I think that must be the greater part of the supernatural guidance that any of us receives. If we want to do His will and we have asked Him to help us do it, I believe that He will order our steps. He will quietly release His thoughts into our receptive minds, and we will make wiser decisions.

I also believe that He makes "deposits" in our minds and spirits. Then when the right time comes, He helps us withdraw what He has placed there. My wife approached her prophetic dreams that way. If she happened to forget a dream, she didn't fret about it. She simply assumed that God had deposited the message of that dream into her spirit and that He would help her recall it if it was important.

Don't Expect to Hear Every Detail

God wants you to walk by faith, not by sight. If He gave you all the details ahead of time, you would walk by sight, not by faith.

So instead of giving you all of the details, God gives you "appetizers." He gives you steps, one step at a time. He gives you encouragement and correction that zero in on the one particular thing that He wants to touch. Most of the time, all you can see is the one step that's in front of you.

As I said in chapter 8, it can be like skipping a stone over the water. God seems to miss a few skips on the way; His stone splashes quickly over A, B, C . . . then H . . . then L, M, N, and so forth. There's nothing wrong with this, even though sometimes we sure wish He'd lay everything out for us in complete detail. He will not do that. He is more interested in establishing and maintaining a culture of dependency with you. He loves you too much to tell you all of the details.

When God Speaks, You May Get Uncomfortable!

Sometimes, following God as closely as we know how, we walk into heartbreak and disappointment. Sometimes we make major mistakes, or at least they seem to be major at the time. Sometimes He tells us to do things that we really do not want to do, such as confessing a sin and asking for forgiveness.

He might send you to a place and not tell you why you're there. You might think you know, and then you find out you're wrong. It does not feel good to die to self, to relinquish your opinions or your well-planned-out schemes.

But if it's God, you will soon learn that it's worth it. You will learn to appreciate the fact that His ways are not the same as your ways (see Isa. 55:8-9). His ways are amazingly good, even if at times they do not seem too pleasant.

Hearing God Speak Should Prompt You to Action

Let me ask you—why are you asking for God's guidance anyway? Most likely you want to know what to *do*. You want it to match up with His will. You want to be safe. You want to make good decisions.

So whatever you hear from Him, it should prompt you to some kind of action. We read in Daniel 11:32, "the people who know their God will display strength and take action" (*NASB*).

This brings me to an important point. Many times people are looking for God's guidance, seemingly in vain. I always ask them, "Did you do the last thing He told you to do?" If they haven't taken action on the last thing that God clearly told them to do, they may need to back up and do it. Or if it's too late to do it now, they may need to ask God's forgiveness and ask Him for another chance. His guidance may be a little different the second time around, but He will send it.

He wants you to hear Him and He wants you to take action. He will help you on both counts.

Divine Guidance Is a Skill to Be Learned
Over a Lifetime

You will never get it all correct. Don't worry about that; it only means that God is much bigger and wiser than you are. You will always have more to learn.

Just when you think you have got it all nailed down tight—"I hear God's voice best if I do these things, and He always speaks to me"—He will seem to change the rules on you. Hearing God is such a part of the supernatural life because the supernatural life is, above all, a *living relationship* with the One who saved you and who is still saving you. Remember, "Seek first His kingdom and His righteousness, and all these things will be added to you" (Matt. 6:33, *NASB*). Seek His face. Seek His heart. Lean on His breast like John the beloved disciple did. Listen for His heartbeat.

Angels—Your Personal
Heavenly Escort

Did you know that most of the answers to your prayers are brought to you by angels? You cannot see them (most of the time), so it is easy to forget about them. But having an awareness of angels, and an appreciation for their work, should be a part of any believer's supernatural life.

John Calvin, the great sixteenth-century French theologian and reformer, wrote, "Angels are ministers and dispensers of the divine bounty towards us. Accordingly, we are told how they watch for our safety, how they undertake our defense, direct our path, and take heed that no evil befall us."[2]

One of my favorite biblical portrayals of angels helping people can be found in the story of Elisha and his servant in 2 Kings:

> When the servant of the man of God got up and went out early the next morning, an army with horses and chariots had surrounded the city. "Oh, my lord, what shall we do?" the servant asked. "Don't be afraid," the prophet answered. "Those who are with us are more than those who are with them." And Elisha prayed, "O Lord, open his eyes so he may see." Then the Lord opened the servant's eyes, and he looked and saw the hills full of horses and chariots of fire all around Elisha (2 Kings 6:15-17).

Elisha's servant is like most of us—he simply was not aware of the possibility of seeing with the eyes of his spirit into the supernatural realm of angels. As he surrendered his senses to the Holy Spirit, he could see the heavenly reality that was otherwise invisible. No longer did he have to rely on someone like Elisha, someone with a special anointing. Now he could see for himself that God had sent more-than-adequate reinforcements.

Angels may be present and yet unperceived at any time. They are not always present, but even when they are, they are not usually noticed by people. Even when one person might be able to perceive them, the next person may not. Those of us who are able to perceive can pray for others to be able to see into this angelic realm, because any of us can grow in our spiritual sensitivity. The same

Holy Spirit lives in each of us. We do not have to be locked in to our limited sensitivity.

As a matter of fact, just as Elisha's servant was astonished when his eyes were opened and he could see the vast angelic army arrayed on the hillsides, so too may you be astonished when you first encounter even one angel. Seeing into the angelic realm will bring a new reality into your life. Suddenly the veil between your familiar, earthly reality and the equally real heavenly reality will become very thin. You may be speechless, stunned, surprised. You will also be grateful, because you will realize that God Himself has sent you the help that you needed at precisely the right time.

Your Response to Angels

You can learn a lot from reading the scriptural accounts of angelic appearances. You can learn what angels do, how they look—and how to respond to them. Angels are mentioned in the Bible 300 times, in both the Old and New Testaments. If you want to live a supernatural life, you certainly cannot disregard them.

How should you respond if you see an angel? They can appear to be pretty intimidating at times. One of the first things most people notice is their size—Extra-Large. Stricken with awe, your first impulse may be to bow down in humble worship (see Col. 2:18). This is understandable, but inappropriate. An angel is a created being, just as you are, a fellow servant of God:

> Now I, John, saw and heard these things. And when
> I heard and saw, I fell down to worship before the

feet of the angel who showed me these things. Then he said to me, "See that you do not do that. For I am your fellow servant, and of your brethren the prophets, and of those who keep the words of this book. Worship God" (Rev. 22:8-9, *NKJV*).

An opposite response—less likely to happen if you are a wholehearted believer—is to scorn or to belittle angels, as if they are imaginary or comical (see Jude 1:8 and 2 Pet. 2:10-11). There is plenty of room for judging the message of an angel, just as you can pass judgment on the truth or falsehood of the words of any human messenger. In fact, we are encouraged to evaluate messages, whether they come from people or angels. But we need to respect angels as fellow servants of God even as we discern whether what we are seeing and hearing is truly from God or possibly tainted by demonic powers (fallen angels).

Angels Are Fellow Servants

As Scripture points out, angels are fellow servants of God. Human beings are His earth-based servants, and angels are His heaven-based ones. God is the Creator of both angels and humans. As the psalmist exclaims: "Praise Him, all His angels; praise Him, all His hosts!" (Ps. 148:2, *NASB*). Above and beyond anything else, angels are devoted to God.

The letter to the Hebrews speaks of angels:

In speaking of the angels he says,
    "He makes his angels winds,
  his servants flames of fire."[3]

Are not all angels ministering spirits sent to serve
those who will inherit salvation? (Heb. 1:7,14).

This passage clearly states it—God has created and
sent angels to serve *us,* the ones who will inherit salvation.
So not only is their service oriented toward God, it is also
oriented toward human beings. Angels work for the benefit of both believers and nonbelievers, who after all may
become believers only with their help.

Through everything angels do runs the same theme:
obedience to God's word:

> Bless the Lord, you His angels,
> > Mighty in strength, who perform His word,
> > Obeying the voice of His word!
> Bless the Lord, all you His hosts,
> > You who serve Him, doing His will
> (Ps. 103:20-21, *NASB*).

It appears that there are two or three ways this works.
Angels sometimes act in accord with a direct command of
God, such as when God commanded Gabriel to deliver a
message to Mary in the Gospel of Luke (see Luke 1:26-28).
Angels also act in response to intercessory prayer. This is
what happened when Daniel was interceding to God for
Israel and Gabriel was sent to him (see Dan. 10:11-12). Another way that angels respond may well involve the utter-
ance of a *rhema* word of God. Angels will not obey a word
from a human being (who is a fellow servant, remember),
but they may well obey God's word through a human as
that person echoes God's word spoken prophetically.

Through the Holy Spirit, a believer can know what God wants to do and can give voice to it, thus enabling angels to be sent into action.

Angelic Ministries

All angels are not alike, and their actions, functions and ministries are not alike either. I have identified at least 14 distinct ways that angels serve.[4]

1. *Angels bring in the presence of God.* A particular phrase is used repeatedly in the Bible: "The angel of His presence" (Isa. 63:9; see also Exod. 13:21; 14:19; 23:20-21; 33:14-15). It seems that when the angel of the Lord's presence shows up, the presence of God does too. This has been interpreted as a theophany of Christ (a pre-incarnate appearance of Jesus, for cases recorded in the Old Testament), which it may well be. But I also believe that when a particular type of angel arrives in a place, that angel ushers in the divine and powerful presence of God Himself. Their arrival signals a tangible difference in the atmosphere. During some of Charles Finney's extended evangelistic meetings, people reported that an encampment of angels came to a spot about a mile away from the meeting site. Finney believed that those angels were there to help release the presence of God into the meetings.

2. *Angels bring God's word.* God sent angels to tell Joseph about Mary's pregnancy and to warn him to take Mary and the baby Jesus to Egypt (see Matt. 1:20; 2:13,19). The angel Gabriel appeared to both Zechariah and Mary to announce the God-sent births of John and Jesus (see Luke 1:19,26-27). Angels delivered a resurrection proclamation to the women at the tomb (see Matt. 18:1-7). This is still happening today. While ministering in Indianapolis a few years ago, I was awakened in the middle of the night by the blast of a shofar. I sat up in bed as the room was electrified with the presence of destiny and purpose. A large, glowing angel glared right into my innermost being and declared, "It's time to begin!" For the next 20 minutes, I witnessed, in an open-eyed vision, the heavens being rolled back to reveal scores upon scores of angels being dispatched to destinations across the globe to do the Father's bidding.

3. *Angels release dreams, revelation and understanding.* The angel Gabriel released understanding to Daniel concerning the end times (see Dan. 8:15-19). The entire book of Revelation was brought to the apostle John by an angel (see Rev. 1:1).

4. *Angels give guidance and direction.* An angel of the Lord told Philip to meet the Ethiopian eunuch on the road (see Acts 8:26). An angel

guided Abraham's servant in his search for a wife for Isaac (see Gen. 24:7). Because of an angel, Paul was sure that God had a further plan for him and that his life and the lives of the others on board the storm-wrecked ship would be spared (see Acts 27:23-24).

5. *Angels bring deliverance.* When an army of Assyrians threatened God's people, one angel killed 185,000 of them (see Isa. 37:36; 2 Kings 19:35). Many of the contemporary stories about angelic activity have to do with deliverance from danger.

6. *Angels provide protection.* In a similar way, angels provide protection in hazardous situations. In what could have been a very serious car accident, a friend of ours was protected by an angel. A policeman said he saw a person (who did not exist) step out of the car with her. Our friend escaped what could have been a fatal crash with only a few bruises. Scripture tells us that angels have charge over children and adult believers (see Matt. 18:10; Pss. 34:7; 91:11-12).

7. *Angels minister upon the death of the saints.* I know this one now from personal experience. On the morning that Michal Ann died, it almost seemed to me that she sprouted wings and flew. There was such peace in that room. I believe that angels were on assignment to take her to her heavenly abode. Psalm 116:15

says, "Precious in the sight of the Lord is the death of his saints." According to Luke 16:22, angels carried the body of the poor man Lazarus to "Abraham's bosom" (that is, heaven) when he died.

8. *Angels impart strength.* In the Garden of Gethsemane, angels were sent to Jesus specifically to minister strength to Him (see Luke 22:43). Earlier, angels had been sent to Him to impart strength after He had been weakened by His 40-day fast in the wilderness (see Matt. 4:11). In the Old Testament, Daniel received strength through an angel's ministrations (see Dan. 10:16).

9. *Angels release God's healing.* Why do you think so many sick people waited around the pool of Bethesda? Because historically, people had been known to receive healing when they stepped into the waters immediately after an angel had stirred them (see John 5:2-4). When healing is "in the house," most likely healing angels are also present. I myself have seen them ministering alongside healing evangelist Mahesh Chavda and in other situations.

10. *Angels minister to God through praise and worship.* Perhaps this form of ministry should have been listed first, since countless angels are ministering in this way at all times (see Rev. 5:11-12; Luke 2:14).

11 *Angels conduct war.* There is a strong indication that the "high praises of God" in the mouths of the saints become supernatural weapons of warfare in the hands of angels (see Ps. 149:5-8). Besides the army of angels that Elisha and his servant saw (see 2 Kings 6:15-17), armies of angels appear in Genesis 32:1-2, Daniel 10:13, Revelation 12:7 and elsewhere in the Bible.

12. *Angels serve as divine watchers.* God's angelic watchmen seem to be increasing their vigilance these days. They look in on the affairs of humankind and take back a report to Headquarters. They are quick to notice and respond to sins against God (see Dan. 4:13,17; Acts 12:23).

13. *Angels release God's judgments.* At the end of time, angels will execute God's final judgments on the earth and its rebellious inhabitants (see Rev. 16:17). In the meantime, they sometimes come to serve warning on disobedient individuals and groups (see Acts 12:23 to find out what an angel did to Herod). Angels brought the judgment of death to Egypt so that Pharaoh would release the children of Israel (see Exod. 12:21-23).

14. *Angels are God's reapers and gatherers.* In the end, angels will gather the lawless and the elect for judgment (see Matt. 13:39-42; 24:31).

Even now, angels are among us to aid in the end-time harvest and the sorting out of the righteous and the unrighteous (see Matt. 13:36-43; Rev. 14:6,14-19).

All of these ministries of angels give evidence to the incomprehensible grandeur of the supernatural realm. As you and I live supernatural lives, we can expect to encounter our fellow servants, the angels, on more than one occasion.

Positioned for an Open Heaven

God wants us to be properly aligned with Him. His purposes for us include living lives that are supernatural so that we are centered on Him and aware of the evidences of His presence. We must move from the side issues to the central ones—as He defines them.

Our human efforts will not suffice. We need help from on high. Like Elisha's servant, we need to have our eyes opened to see the invisible help that surrounds us already, and we need to call out for reinforcements. God will send help from His throne room and He will help us position ourselves to receive it.

More than ever, in these end times, we need to be able to hear God's still, small voice. We need to learn to use all of our senses to see, hear, smell and touch the reality of His kingdom. He wants to open the heavens and come down. You will hear people talk about "open heavens," when the veil is especially thin and He manifests Himself in particularly vivid ways.

He is the Creator. He creates open heavens just as He has created the inhabitants of His kingdom, which include you and me. Let's respond to Him, and let's encourage each other to keep on responding to Him. He will help us.

Review

Living a supernatural life entails being able to use your Spirit-enhanced senses to discover what God is saying. The supernatural realm is vast, and we have only glimpsed snapshots of it when we see God's will performed through prayer and angelic assistance.

1. Do you think that you yourself can hear God? Why or why not?

2. In your personal experience, how have you seen angels at work?

3. As you have read this chapter, has some aspect of it captured your attention in a special way? See if you can put into words a new resolve to learn more, listen to God better or take a particular action.

Part IV
All Things Are Possible

As we move through our lives, we encounter many difficulties. Buffeted by tough circumstances, we tend to take refuge in all sorts of man-made hiding places.

We are trying to do the best we can—under the circumstances. But, as Bob Mumford used to say, "What are you doing under *there*?" When we take things into our own hands, we remain under the circumstances instead of on top of them.

Evaluating our circumstances with our limited understanding, we too often fail to see evidence of God's mercy and we cannot walk in abundant faith. With the man whose son was not yet healed, we say, "Lord, I believe; help my unbelief!" (Mark 9:24, *NKJV*).

He is both able and willing to help us in every way, because He does love us. He has not yet plucked us out of this troubled world to take us home, but He has supplied us with everything we need to prevail over our circumstances and to hold our ground. What Jesus told His disciples is true of us—when we are living the supernatural life: "With God all things are possible" (Matt. 19:26).

Chapter 10

He Sets the Captives Free

You were born into the middle of a supernatural battle, as we discussed in the first chapter. Even as a new believer, you started to encounter opposition. Soon you began to realize that you would need help. You read your Bible, prayed and listened to seasoned battle veterans. You began to learn the ropes.

Although your spiritual life has gone up and down, by now you have assembled, with the help of the Holy Spirit, a full suit of heavenly armor, which you have been learning how to wear (see Eph. 6:12-13). If you look down, you see that you have your feet shod with the gospel of peace. Your head is covered with the strong helmet of salvation. You are wearing both the belt of truth and the breastplate of righteousness. You are holding the shield of faith in one hand and the sword of the Spirit (the Word) in the other.

Your armor is intended for two purposes: both defensive and offensive. It defends and protects you from the blows of the enemy. It also equips you to stand firm, resisting the enemy without capitulation, and it enables you to execute offensive battlefield strategies that your Commander initiates. In the end, not only does your armor give you supernatural protection, but it also helps you do your part to bring in the Kingdom.

None of this happens apart from your "normal" life, whatever that is. This *is* your normal life, and it is naturally supernatural. Regardless of what people see you doing 24 hours a day, you are serving as a full-time soldier in the army called the Church. You have enlisted for life.

I have an adjusted view on the supernatural life. I now believe that it takes as much supernatural help to *maintain* my ground as it does to take new territory. (The reason I have this adjusted view is because I have less hair on my head than I did 10 years ago.) I think you can agree with me that, at times, simply holding your ground constitutes a victory. Maintaining what you have attained is an achievement—maintaining your integrity, maintaining your boundaries, maintaining your belief that all things work together for good for those who love God and are called according to His purpose (see Rom. 8:28).

Of course there are definite seasons when you plough ahead and take new territory. Usually, you will not be able to do it solo; most offensive efforts happen in collaboration with others. One primary reason is because your armor does not cover your backside, and you are vulnerable if you fight alone. We need each other (see Eccles. 4:9-12). In a very real way, we are weapons of spiritual warfare for each other, guarding each other from harm.

Our supernatural weapons do not resemble earthly weapons:

> For though we walk (live) in the flesh, we are not carrying on our warfare according to the flesh and using mere human weapons. For the weapons of our warfare are not physical [weapons of flesh and

blood], but they are mighty before God for the overthrow and destruction of strongholds (2 Cor. 10:3-4, *AMP*).

A good portion of our supernatural living involves the overthrow of ungodly strongholds, so that the one true Stronghold, Jesus Christ, can be our strong tower of defense and beacon of hope (see Pss. 9:9; 18:2; 27:1; 37:39; 43:2; 52:7; 144:2).

The Strong Man

Ungodly strongholds can be broken down and plundered. First, though, you need to bind up the stronghold-keeper, who is the "strong man" Jesus referred to when He said, "How can anyone enter a strong man's house and carry off his possessions unless he first ties up the strong man? Then he can rob his house" (Matt. 12:29).

The strong man is a demonic force. (C. Peter Wagner believes the term refers specifically to Beelzebub, a high-ranking demonic principality who seems to have territorial authority.) He captures and imprisons unsaved people, whom he strives to keep in subjugation.

The strong man is strong, but there is One who is stronger, and His name is Jesus Christ. He accomplishes His mission by the power of His Holy Spirit. Even when the people accused Him of casting out demons by the power of Beelzebub, He pointed to the Spirit as the active force:

If I drive out demons by the finger of God, then the kingdom of God has come to you. When a strong man, fully armed, guards his own house, his possessions are safe. But when someone stronger attacks and overpowers him, he takes away the armor in which the man trusted and divides up the spoils (Luke 11:20-22).

(The "finger of God" is understood to refer to the Holy Spirit, especially since in the parallel passage, Matthew 12:18, Jesus says, "If I cast out demons by the Spirit of God . . .")

The truth is: "greater is He who is in you than he who is in the world" (1 John 4:4, *NASB*). Regardless of whether the "finger of God" operates through Jesus Himself as it did in the Gospels, or through you or me as it does today, the Holy Spirit is powerful enough to overcome any strong man. The Spirit of God is always looking for ways to bring in the Kingdom. He works through believers who cooperate with His supernatural bondage-breaking activity.

Discovering Enemy Access Points

In order to overthrow the enemy's strongholds, our first strategy must be to uncover his access points. What gave the enemy legal access to this person, this group of people or this region? Demonic spirits have no true authority to influence an area without permission. All over the world, existing conditions give the powers of the air plenty of legal authority to remain and operate against God's purpose and the welfare of humanity. What are some of these conditions that can serve both as personal access points and corporate or territorial access points?

- *Fighting, anger, hatred, cursing and unforgiveness.* The Bible says, "Whoever rewards evil for good, evil will not depart from his house" (Prov. 17:13, *NKJV*, see also 1 Pet. 3:9). We are urged to forgive others (see Matt. 18:21-35), to come to the Lord's table with clean hearts (see 1 Cor. 11:27-30), and to remain in a proper relationship with those in authority (see Rom. 13:1-2).

- *Witchcraft.* The Bible is very clear—witchcraft, which includes divination and sorcery, and which is practiced by many people today, is an open door to demonic forces (see Deut. 18:10-12).

- *Substance abuse—alcohol, drugs and more.* Substance abuse is nothing more than witchcraft under a deceptively "fun" disguise. The word in the Bible that is translated "sorcerers," in Greek is *pharmakeus* or *pharmakos,* related to the word *pharmakon,* which means an herbal remedy, a drug or a poison (see Rev. 21:8 and 22:15).

- *Adultery, sodomy, perversion and all other sexual sins.* All sexual sins represent distortions of the God-given sexual drive. As individuals and cultures—even within the Church—we have opened the door to the enemy through sexual sins (see Lev. 18 and 20; Deut. 23:17; Rom. 1:24-28).

- *Banishment of prayer and Bible reading from schools and the public sphere.* When God was kicked out of schools and other public places, the god of secular humanism came in to fill the void. Human beings assume God's position to solve problems, making themselves out to be gods.

· *Murder and the shedding of innocent blood.* Besides wars and violent crime, we have opened the door to Satan's forces by our national acceptance of abortion, which has allowed more than 50 million children to be legally murdered since 1973.

· *Temples to pagan religions.* This applies not only to ancient "high places" of demonic or occult worship (see 2 Kings 17:11; Ps. 78:58; Jer. 19:5; 32:35), but also to culturally accepted "temples" such as Freemasonry and harmless-looking cults.

· *Idolatry.* Simply stated, idolatry is the worship of anything or anyone besides God. People become slaves to whatever they worship (see 1 Cor. 10:19-20).

These are representative categories of "access points"—sins that open the door wide to the enemy and that allow him to establish strongholds in the land. With these in mind, let's tackle the side of supernatural life that has to do with tearing down the strongholds that hold us captive. Wherever you need to repent personally, do so. Ask for help if you need to. The supernatural life is meant to be a life of increasing freedom, and the Holy Spirit brings us the help we need for victory over the strong man, because He is the Strongest One of all!

Your Personal Warfare Strategy

In the supernatural life, spiritual warfare is waged daily. Much of the time, it is waged silently, without fireworks, as believers just move through their lives with integrity and peace:

> While your loyalty and obedience is known to all, so that I rejoice over you, I would have you well versed and wise as to what is good and inno-cent and guileless as to what is evil. And the God of peace will soon crush Satan under your feet (Rom. 16:19-20, *AMP*).

Simple submission to God is a foundational strategy. So is basic resistance: "Submit yourselves, then, to God. Resist the devil, and he will flee from you" (Jas. 4:7; see also 1 Pet. 5:5-8).

As you resist the enemy's sinful suggestions, you will want to use the sword of the Spirit, the Word of God (see Eph. 6:17). That is what Jesus did when the devil tempted Him in the wilderness (see Luke 4:1-13). You wield the sword of the Word by speaking it out, either from memory or by reading it aloud, declaring the truth into the atmosphere. Just as you have to take up the full armor of God yourself, you have to wield the sword yourself; the Spirit will not do it for you. He furnishes the weaponry. You must pick it up and use it.

Jesus said that one of the signs that would distinguish believers is that they would cast out demons outright (see Mark 16:17). There again, the Holy Spirit is not going to do it for you. He will help you know what to do, but you have to step into the situation with faith and open your mouth.

Take Away His Armor

Spiritual warfare strategies should be standard for every Spirit-filled believer. As you learn how to make them a part of your supernatural life, you will discover many of the techniques that make such strategies successful. In essence, these are life skills for the supernatural life. They deprive the strong man of his armor so that you can win. Here are a number of specific ways to "deactivate" the enemy in your life:

- Confess your sin and identify with others' sin (identificational repentance; see 1 John 1:9).
- Pull down strongholds of lies in your mind (see 2 Cor. 10:3-5).
- Control your tongue (see Jas. 2:19; 3:1-10).
- Live to love; make love your aim (see 1 Cor. 13:1-8; Jas. 3:13-18).
- Refuse pride. Humble yourself (see Phil. 2:1-8; 1 Pet. 5:6; Jas. 4:6).
- Develop self-control. Exercise the fruit of faith (see Gal. 5:22).
- Confess your sins to others (see Jas. 5:16).
- Forgive always and quickly (see Mark 11:25).
- Walk in the light (see 1 John 1:5-7).
- Refuse fear and worry (see 2 Tim. 1:7; Matt. 6:25-26).
- Refuse isolationism and self-pity (see Heb. 10:23-25).

- Flee from lust (see 2 Tim. 2:22; Prov. 5).
- Avoid foolish arguments (see 2 Tim. 2:23-26).
- Control your appetites (see Rom. 12:1; Phil. 3:17-19).
- Act in the opposite spirit (see Rom. 12:20-21).
- Allow no common ground with the enemy (see John 14:30).

Every one of these intentional actions deprives the enemy of part of his armor or one of his weapons against you. For example, when you refuse isolationism, you choose fellowship. Fellowship is good for you, and it diffuses self-pity. Your fellow believers remind you of the truth, and they love you. What better way to regain your emotional and spiritual footing? By refusing to remain isolated, you have deprived the enemy of some of his darts of discouragement; you have silenced his negative insinuations, and more.

Put On the Full Armor of God

As you act to take away some of your enemy's weaponry, make sure that all of your own armor is secure.

Check to make sure that *truth* is buckled firmly in place: "Your word is truth" (John 17:17). Take your "pulse" of *peace* (see Phil. 4:6-7; 1 Pet. 5:7). You will have peace if you are doing the current will of God. Reach up and re-situate the *hope* that you wear like a helmet (see 1 Thess. 5:8). Keep on keeping on; "continue to work out your *salvation* with fear and trembling" (Phil. 2:12, emphasis added).

Look at yourself in the mirror of the Spirit to see if you are properly clothed in *righteousness*, which is easy to wear because Jesus gave it to you; you did not create it through your own works and striving for perfection (see Matt. 5:6). As you stand there in the light, ask yourself, "Am I living by *faith*?" It is so easy not to. Faith must be cultivated, developed, exercised. Faith is a culture. Faith is also a fruit of the Spirit and a gift. Your faith is a measure of your overall spiritual health (see Mark 11:22; Rom. 10:17; 12:2).

Are you *standing* in faith? Paul told the Ephesians, "Therefore put on the full armor of God, so that when the day of evil comes, you may be able to stand your ground, and after you have done everything, to stand" (Eph. 6:13).

Know Your Weapons

Remind yourself often of the wide range of specialized weapons you have at your disposal. They were issued to you when you enlisted in God's army, so don't forget about them or neglect them. Very soon, you may need to pull one of them out and use it. You have the Word as a sword, but you also have a whole lot more than that.

The sword of the Spirit. "For the word of God is living and active. Sharper than any double-edged sword, it penetrates even to dividing soul and spirit, joints and marrow; it judges the thoughts and attitudes of the heart" (Heb. 4:12).

The name of Jesus. "Therefore God also has highly exalted Him and given Him the name which is above every name, that at the name of Jesus every knee should bow, of those in heaven, and of those on earth, and of those under the earth, and that every tongue should confess that Jesus Christ is Lord, to the glory of God the Father" (Phil. 2:9-11, *NKJV*).

The blood of Jesus. Taking the Lord's Supper (Communion) is one of the greatest tools for displacing darkness and declaring along with Jesus, "It is finished." The ninth chapter of the book of Hebrews explains the significance of the blood of Jesus: "In fact, the law requires that nearly everything be cleansed with blood, and without the shedding of blood there is no forgiveness" (Heb. 9:22).

The keys of the kingdom. Jesus said, "I will give you the keys of the kingdom of heaven; whatever you bind on earth will be bound in heaven, and whatever you loose on earth will be loosed in heaven" (Matt. 16:19; see also Matt. 18:18).

The power of forgiveness. Jesus told the story of the unforgiving servant, and then He ended with this statement: "This is how my heavenly Father will treat each of you unless you forgive your brother from your heart" (Matt. 18:35).

The gifts of the Holy Spirit. "Now to each one the manifestation of the Spirit is given for the common good. To one there is given through the Spirit the message of wisdom, to another the message of knowledge by means of the same Spirit, to another faith by the same Spirit, to another gifts of healing by that one Spirit, to another miraculous powers, to another prophecy, to another distinguishing between spirits, to another speaking in different kinds of tongues, and to still another the interpretation of tongues" (1 Cor. 12:7-10).

Prayer. Jesus said, "Ask and it will be given to you; seek and you will find; knock and the door will be opened to you" (Matt. 7:7).

Praying in tongues. "The Spirit helps us in our weakness. We do not know what we ought to pray for, but the Spirit himself intercedes for us with groans that words cannot express. And he who searches our hearts knows the mind of the Spirit, because the Spirit intercedes for the saints in accordance with God's will" (Rom. 8:26-27).

Angels. "No harm will befall you, no disaster will come near your tent. For he will command his angels concerning you to guard you in all your ways; they will lift you up in their hands, so that you will not strike your foot against a stone" (Ps. 91:10-12).

Praise. "Let the saints be joyful in glory; let them sing aloud on their beds. Let the high praises of God be in their mouth, and a two-edged sword in their hand, to execute vengeance on the nations, and punishments on the peoples; to bind their kings with chains, and their nobles with fetters of iron; to execute on them the written judgment—this honor have all His saints" (Ps. 149:5-9, *NKJV*).

Worship. "Jesus said to him, 'Away from me, Satan! For it is written: "Worship the Lord your God, and serve him only"'" (Matt. 4:10). "Therefore, since we are receiving a kingdom that cannot be shaken, let us be thankful, and so worship God acceptably with reverence and awe" (Heb. 12:28).

Fasting. When the disciples tried to set a demonized boy free, Jesus told them, "But this kind does not go out except by prayer and fasting" (Matt. 17:21). Fasting is also a weapon because it makes a person humble (see Joel 2:12).

Discerning of spirits. "But to each one is given the manifestation of the [Holy] Spirit . . . to one . . . to another the ability to discern and distinguish between [the utterances of true] spirits [and false ones]" (1 Cor. 12:7-8,10, *AMP*).

Prophecy. "Follow the way of love and eagerly desire spiritual gifts, especially the gift of prophecy" (1 Cor. 14:1).

"Timothy, my son, I give you this instruction in keeping with the prophecies once made about you, so that by following them you may fight the good fight" (1 Tim. 1:18).

Agreement. "I tell you that if two of you on earth agree about anything you ask for, it will be done for you by my Father in heaven" (Matt. 18:19).

Commands. For example, "Get behind me, Satan!" (Matt. 16:23).

The community of believers. As I noted earlier, the Body of Christ itself is a weapon of spiritual warfare, simply because individuals love, support, protect and strengthen one another. "They devoted themselves to the apostles' teaching and to the fellowship, to the breaking of bread and to prayer" (Acts 2:42).

Humility. "Yes, all of you be submissive to one another, and be clothed with humility, for 'God resists the proud, but gives grace to the humble'" (1 Pet. 5:5, *NKJV*).

The gift of faith. "Since we have the same spirit of faith, according to what is written, 'I believed and therefore I spoke,' we also believe and therefore speak" (2 Cor. 4:13, *NKJV*).

Grace. "'Not by might nor by power, but by My Spirit,' says the Lord of hosts. 'Who are you, O great mountain? . . . you shall become a plain! and he shall bring forth the capstone with shouts of "Grace, grace to it!"'" (Zech. 4:6-7, *NKJV*).

The Lord Himself. "What, then, shall we say in response to this? If God is for us, who can be against us? . . . Who shall separate us from the love of Christ? Shall trouble or hardship or persecution or famine or nakedness or danger or sword? . . . No, in all these things we are more than conquerors through him who loved us. For I am convinced that neither death nor life, neither angels nor demons, neither the present nor the future, nor any powers, neither height nor depth, nor anything else in all creation, will be able to separate us from the love of God that is in Christ Jesus our Lord" (Rom. 8:31,35,37-39).

The presence of God. One time, as I was in worship, the Spirit said to me, "I will teach you to release the highest weapon of spiritual warfare: the majesty of My great presence. He is the highest weapon of spiritual warfare." "And the Lord said, My Presence shall go with you, and I will give you rest" (Exod. 33:14, *AMP*).

The Holy Spirit will teach you how to use all of the weapons He has given you, and He will enable you to stand firm against the forces of darkness. Whenever necessary in your supernaturally natural life, the Spirit will enable you to not only stand firm against the assaults of evil, but actually disarm them. You yourself can experience deliverance and freedom, and in turn, you can deliver captives, break curses, change ungodly beliefs and reform generational sin patterns.

Review

The good news is that you can live a supernatural life with God. The bad news is that you have a personal enemy who is out to destroy you (see John 10:10). The *best* news is that "He who is in you is greater than he who is in the world" (1 John 4:4, *NKJV*)!

Not only do you have a personal enemy, but you have a personal Lord who knows everything at all times and who, therefore, has a strategy that is tailor-made to fit your situation. As you learn about the principles of His kingdom, you are better able to take your place in the Lord's army of believers, the Church.

When Jesus established His Church, He promised that the gates of hell would not prevail against it (see Matt. 16:18). He commissioned us to do battle "against principalities, against powers, against the rulers of the darkness of this age, against spiritual hosts of wickedness in the heavenly places" (Eph. 6:12, *NKJV*). His plan for your life—your *supernatural* life—is that you will be able to do your part to help Jesus fulfill His purpose in being born as a man, which is to destroy the works of the devil (see 1 John 3:8) and to set the captives free (see Eph. 4:8; Col. 2:15).

1. How have you experienced the spiritual battle, personally?

2. How have you allied yourself with other members of the Body of Christ, the Church? How could you strengthen those bonds?

3. What part of this chapter made you pause because it struck a chord with your spirit? Take time right now to pray about it so that you can become stronger in the Spirit.

Chapter 11

The Children's Bread

I am so grateful for the privilege of living the supernatural life. Instead of living just an ordinary human life, you and I get to taste heaven before we get there.

What will it be like in heaven? One of the things we know about heaven is that there is no pain, sorrow, death or sickness there:

> God will wipe away every tear from their eyes; and death shall be no more, neither shall there be anguish (sorrow and mourning) nor grief nor pain any more, for the old conditions and the former order of things have passed away (Rev. 21:4, *AMP*).

Therefore, part of tasting heaven before we get there is being able to sample healing—of any disease or condition—right here.

The reason I have called this chapter "The Children's Bread" is because of the following story; that phrase has come to mean "healing":

> Then she came and worshiped Him, saying, "Lord, help me!"
>
> But He answered and said, "It is not good to take the children's bread and throw it to the little dogs."

And she said, "Yes, Lord, yet even the little dogs eat the crumbs which fall from their masters' table."

Then Jesus answered and said to her, "O woman, great is your faith! Let it be to you as you desire." And her daughter was healed from that very hour (Matt. 15:25-28, *NKJV*).

As we bow before Him in worship and supplication, Jesus brings healing to our lives, too. He invites us to press in for it, and our effort will not be in vain, for "He is a rewarder of those who diligently seek Him" (Heb. 11:6, *NKJV*).

History of Healing in the Church

Throughout Christian history we have seen men and women who have carried an anointing to release the healing power of God so that people could be set free from sicknesses.

For the first hundred years of the Church, the time known as the apostolic era, healing was common. Irenaeus (A.D. 125–202), who was an early bishop and theologian, wrote:

For some do certainly and truly drive out devils, so that those who have been cleansed from evil spirits frequently both believe in Christ and join themselves to the Church. Others have foreknowledge of things to come; they see vision, and utter prophetic expression. Others still heal the sick by laying their hands upon them and

they are made whole. Yea, moreover . . . the dead
have been raised up, and remained among us for
many years.[1]

As we read Irenaeus's report, we recognize that the
Christians under his oversight were living naturally supernatural lives. But after the abundant supernatural
manifestations of the first century, the Church went
through a prolonged season when healing and other
miracles almost seemed to die out, and large numbers of
believers never saw or experienced anything like God's
healing power.

Cessationist teaching further paralyzed faith in the
healing gifts. Cessationists believe that the acts of Jesus
in power and the use of the gifts of His Spirit ceased after the last apostles died and the last book of the canon
of Scripture was written. They say that we no longer re-
quired the miraculous gifts of the Spirit once we had
the fullness of God's counsel and will revealed in the
written Word. But the main character of the Bible declares, "Truly, truly, I say to you, he who believes in Me,
the works that I do, he will do also; and greater works
than these he will do; because I go to the Father" (John
14:12, *NASB*).

The Vision of the Man of Fire
I want to tell you about part of my own personal supernatural walk, because it involves an experience of healing that expanded into a vision of Jesus, the Healer.

I was in a time of personal crisis—I had been diag-
nosed with non-Hodgkin's lymphoma, a form of cancer.

Even before I knew I had cancer, the Holy Spirit had told me that a surprise was going to come my way in the month of October and that I should keep my travel schedule free then. In August, I discovered a cancerous growth. Along with prayers for healing, I began to receive radiation treatments.

Then in October, an African gentleman came to town. He works with Iris Ministries with Rolland and Heidi Baker, and he has been used to pray for healings and miracles and to raise people from the dead. In fact, he has also been given the ability to preach in languages that he has not learned, a gift of tongues that is used to preach the gospel in places where no one can preach in that language. This gentleman's name is Supresa—in English, it's "Surprise"!

Pastor Surprise came to pray with me. He is just a simple believing man, commissioned by God, and his praying is uncomplicated. At first nothing happened. Then I felt heat start rotating and going through my circulatory system. I could feel it moving, and then it would stop. It would land in a certain part of my body and concentrate there. I was wondering, *Wow, I wonder what's going on?* I started perspiring.

Then I was catapulted into an interactive vision, and I saw a man standing in fire. He motioned for me to step into the fire with him. Then I realized that it was Jesus. As I cooperated and went into the fire with Him, I heard Him speak to me. He said, "With every wound, I obtained a special level of healing for My people." Then He proceeded to show me each of His wounds, interpreting every one of them and describing the special healing that each one had obtained.

He showed me His head, and I saw where the crown of thorns had sat. He said, "I have obtained, with this wound, healing for every realm of mental disease."

He showed me His back. I saw the lacerations from when He was whipped before He was crucified. I remembered the words from Isaiah: "by His stripes we are healed" (Isa. 53:5, *NKJV*; also see 1 Pet. 2:24). These lacerations didn't look like stripes. They were deep, much more gruesome than they were in Mel Gibson's movie *The Passion of the Christ*. In each one of these slashes, I saw words written. I saw words like "leukemia" and "arthritis." Each one had obtained a special level of healing for that particular disease.

Then He turned to His feet and He showed me the wounds from the nails. He told me that they had obtained for Him a special level of healing for every paralysis. He showed me the wounds in His hands and He said something fascinating: "Did you know that most diseases are transferred through the hand?" Then He said, "I have obtained healing for every transferable disease through the nail prints in My hands."

Last of all, He took me to His side where He had been pierced through with the spear. He told me that He died of a broken heart, and that He had obtained a special level of healing for everyone who is brokenhearted. He showed me again all of the wounds: head, back, feet, hands and side, interpreting each one for me and telling me that He had obtained healing for the whole person.

Through that encounter, faith was imparted to me. I was touched by the supernatural power of God, never to be the same. I want to keep before me that revelation of our supernatural God, never lowering my expectations to match others' or to match a temporary circumstance.

As a result of this encounter, the growth, which had reached the size of a cluster of grapes, dissolved. I was still scheduled for five more treatments. I had to have my oncologist and radiologist check and double-check that it was really gone. They had never seen such a thing before. They were amazed! I was amazed!

At the same time, I had so much burned skin from the earlier treatments that I had been using special oils and wearing loose clothing. It hurt a lot. The growth was gone, but my skin was still burned and peeling. In another meeting, a man had a word of knowledge that someone had a serious burn, and he indicated the area where mine was. I received prayer, went home, and didn't really think about it overnight. The next morning I got up and took a shower. Lo and behold, I didn't have the burn anymore—it was like I had baby skin!

Two miracles. I can't explain it—except to say that healing is the children's bread!

Healing Is Holistic

The more deeply you explore the process of healing, the more you understand that healing concerns every part of a human being—body, mind and spirit. In one word, healing needs to be "holistic." People are not compartmentalized. What happens to your mind and spirit affects your body, and vice versa.

In addition, we should not isolate healing that occurs through natural or medical means from that which comes through miraculous means. In our effort to minister supernaturally, we should have no reason to neglect or put down natural means. Physical illnesses are often caused or exacerbated by emotional or spiritual (even demonic) elements. The complex interrelationships between the various types of sicknesses, the parts of the human makeup, and different kinds of healing make it imperative to embrace a holistic view of the process.

We will never be able to understand it completely; so, since each of us has been commissioned to heal (see Matt. 10:1-8; 28:18-20), we must cultivate a relationship with the Holy Spirit so that we can see what the Father is doing and cooperate with it. Because Jesus came as a man and demonstrated that one could heal, we should follow in His steps.

Jesus always combined healing with the proclamation of the kingdom of God (see, for example, Matt. 4:23; 12:28; Luke 9:1-2; 10:1,9). By healing the sick, Jesus defeated Satan and demonstrated His rule. (In the New Testament, ill health was seen as an extension of and as a result of sin, evil in origin and therefore representing the kingdom of Satan.) Healing is associated with repentance from sin and conflict with Satan. Frequently, health is determined by individual righteousness (see Mark 2:1-2; John 5:1-11; Jas. 5:14-16). Cooperating with disobedience and sin will open a person up to weakness, sickness and death (see Acts 5:1-11; 1 Cor. 11:27-32).

Divine holistic healing, therefore, is more than even physical and spiritual wholeness, because it touches on every aspect of the human life that can come under the power or influence of Satan. Divine healing is supernatural, even when it involves natural processes. It includes the following aspects:

- Forgiveness of sins
- Restoration from sickness
- Breaking the hold of poverty and oppressive social structures
- Deliverance from demonic power and influence
- Raising the dead

All of these are signs of the presence and the power of God's kingdom (see Luke 7:22-23).

Why Did Jesus Heal?

In general, we can say that Jesus healed to demonstrate the good news of the coming of the Kingdom (see Matt. 9:35). But, in order to make the "children's bread" easier to reach, we can break this down further. When Jesus healed, He responded to a wide range of Kingdom concerns, the following of which I can see in Scripture:

- Jesus healed simply because He was asked (see Mark 7:31-37).
- Jesus healed in response to faith (see Matt. 9:20-22).
- Jesus healed to testify of Himself and His message (see Acts 2:22).
- Jesus healed to open doors to evangelism (see Acts 9:20-43).
- Jesus healed to honor His commitment to the Church (see Jas. 5:14-16).
- Jesus healed so that He and His Father could be glorified (see John 11:1-4).

• Jesus healed because He had compassion (see Mark 1:40-41).

Through the power and presence of His Holy Spirit, He is still healing today. If you have not already experienced His healing power, before long in your supernatural walk with Him, you will!

Healing in the Atonement

Faith in personal salvation is a supernatural thing. Even believers who take issue with divine healing do not have any trouble believing that Jesus atoned for our sin when He died on the cross. ("Atone" means to reconcile, to appease, to expiate or to make propitiation.)

Is the cross sufficient, not only to take away our sin but also our diseases? Various well-known Christians have considered this issue, and they have reached the same conclusion: Yes, it is. Here are some of their observations:

> In the atonement of Christ there seems to be a foundation laid for faith in bodily healing . . . that we have Christ set before us as the sickness bearer as well as the sin bearer of His people. . . . The yoke of His cross by which he lifted up our inequities took hold also of our diseases . . . Christ endured vicariously our diseases as well as our inequities.[2] (A. J. Gordon, Baptist cofounder of Gordon-Conwell Theological Seminary)

> In Is. 53:4-5 the very mirror image of the coming Redeemer . . . is surely the promise of healing, the very strongest possible statement of complete

redemption from pain and sickness by His life and death. . . . Therefore as He hath borne our sins, Jesus Christ has also borne away, and carried off our sicknesses; yea and even our pains, so that abiding in him, we may be fully delivered from both sickness and pain. Thus by his stripes we are healed.[3] (A. B. Simpson, founder of the Christian and Missionary Alliance)

The greatest barrier to the faith of many seeking bodily healing in our day is the uncertainty in their minds as to it being the will of God to heal *all*. Nearly everyone knows that God does heal *some*, but there is much in modern theology that keeps the people from knowing what the Bible clearly teaches—that healing is provided for all. It is impossible to boldly claim, by faith, a blessing which we are not sure God offers because the power of God can be claimed only where the will of God is known.[4] (F. F. Bosworth, healing evangelist)

Isaiah said of the Christ who was to come: He was wounded for our transgressions, he was bruised for our iniquities (there is the sin question); and with his stripes we are healed (there is the sickness question), thus showing again that provision has been made for deliverance from both sin and sickness.[5] (T. L. Osborn, healing evangelist)

If Christ bore the penalty for my sins, then I do not have to bear it. If Christ bore my sicknesses, then I do not have to suffer it. His sacrifice is

complete, nothing lacking. The atonement for
our sins was effected on the cross. With his stripes
we are healed. Healing for our bodies, as well as
healing for our souls was provided by our Lord
through His atoning death. It is now up to us to
accept the finished work of Christ and appropriate by faith the forgiveness or healing that we
need.[6] (Hugh Jeter, Assemblies of God pastor)

Healing Is Supernaturally Natural

You cannot dissect the supernatural life any more than
you can dissect the natural life, because the component
parts are too well integrated. Healing—healing of every
type of human ailment—is at the heart of the supernatural life because it has such a bearing on a person's ability
to carry on living a life of faith, day after day.

If you're physically sick, it's hard to live by faith. Still
more difficult is living by faith when you are crippled with
spiritual or emotional hurts or if you are troubled by
demons. That's why, to make it possible for you to live a
supernatural life with Him and to bring His kingdom into
the darkness of your heart, the Spirit of Jesus offers you
healing for everything: healing of your body, healing of
your spirit, healing of your emotions, healing of your
mind, healing of your relationships, strength and comfort
when you are dying, and sometimes even healing from
death (i.e., resurrection).

At times His healing involves deliverance from evil
spirits. Frequently, it takes place through the natural
processes of healing that He built into the universe.

Usually the process of healing happens over time. (After all, you would probably disintegrate if He healed everything that needs healing in an instant.) Occasionally you will see a healing miracle, which is instantaneous, but most healings are progressive. When you are seeking for healing over a period of time, you are seeking Him out, because He is the Source. While you are seeking Him, you are growing in the supernatural life.

Here is a reprise of the types of healing I listed above:

Healing of your body. Bodily sickness is rooted in physical factors, either organic or functional disorders. Therefore, healing of the body means changing and restoring normal physical functions.

Blind Bartimaeus couldn't see, but there is no indication that it was a sin issue or a deliverance issue (see Mark 10:46-52). Parts of his eyes just were not working right. When Jesus passed by, he sought His help, and Jesus healed him so he could see.

Healing of your spirit. Spiritual sickness is mainly caused by sin. Healing of your spirit means renewal and restoration of your spiritual life as your relationship with Him is restored. The deepest kind of healing is the forgiveness of sins, which Jesus supplies in response to repentance. When you received His salvation, your spirit began to be restored. As you have been growing in your walk of faith, you are uncovering the need for further restoration of your spirit.

Further healing is always available; it is never too late. You know that "he who began a good work in you will carry it on to completion until the day of Christ Jesus" (Phil. 1:6).

Healing of your emotions. God heals your hurt-filled memories and your damaged emotions. While sickness of your spirit is caused by what you do, sickness of the emotions is generally caused by what has been done to you by others or by difficult circumstances. Depending on how you have reacted to your past experiences, you can end up with weak or wounded emotions, which in turn can lead to sins, depression, a sense of worthlessness and inferiority, unreasonable fears and anxieties, psychosomatic illnesses, and so forth.

Healing of your emotions touches not only your immediate emotions, but also your memories that feed those emotions. Often the spiritual problems that you inherited from your family will be touched and healed. Healing of the emotions is also called "inner healing," and it is a discipline of digging deeply, under the guidance of the Holy Spirit, to discover the roots of your emotional problems and then bring them to death on the cross.[7]

After Peter's denial of Jesus, the Lord came to him specifically to heal his shattered heart. Just as Peter had denied His Lord three distinct times, so the Lord Jesus spoke to him three distinct times, restoring him to full discipleship and sonship (see Matt. 26:33-35,69-75; John 21:15-17). Jesus, as you know, came to "preach the gospel to the poor . . . to heal the brokenhearted, to preach deliverance to the captives, and recovering of sight to the blind, to set at liberty them that are bruised, to preach the acceptable year of the Lord" (Luke 4:18-19, quoting Isa. 61:1, *KJV*).

Healing of your mind. Your brain is an organ of your body, and sometimes it needs physical healing. Other times, it needs emotional healing too. Also, sometimes the healing of your mind involves deliverance from the influence of evil spirits. Mental illness caused by demons can have the same symptoms as spiritual, emotional and physical sickness. This can be hard for us to accept, but if we can believe that our sins can be forgiven, why can't we believe that we can be delivered from evil spirits?

The healing in the "children's bread" story that I quoted at the beginning of this chapter was a deliverance. The demon had tormented the poor girl, and the situation seemed hopeless. Her mother pled with Jesus, "Lord, Son of David, have mercy on me! My daughter is suffering terribly from demon-possession" (Matt. 15:22). Possibly some of her suffering was physical, but a good part of any suffering is emotional and mental. Once deliverance happened, she was in her right mind, permanently (see also Mark 7:24-30).

Healing of your relationships. The violation of godly precepts results in damage to the societal aspect of our lives and in broken relationships. Unhealed people hurt other people. Hurting people hurt other people.

As a result, all of us need healing of our relationships. This type of healing can be applied with particular value within the marriage relationship. Healing of your relationships comes with an exchange of forgiveness and a reapplication of the godly principles that were violated. It goes without saying that harmonious interpersonal relationships contribute to the health of the whole Church and community.

Strength and comfort when you are dying. This one might seem to be a surprising application of the idea of "healing," but that is only because we don't discuss it very often. This kind of healing is the same as comfort. The idea is to bring people through the experience of death—both the one who is dying and those who are bereaved. Jesus said, "Blessed are those who mourn, for they will be comforted" (Matt. 5:4).

Sometimes, of course, the Lord gives a reprieve from death. He did it with the centurion's servant in Matthew 8:5-13, and He did it again with the nobleman's son in John 4:46-53.

Healing from death. Healing from death is the same as resurrection from death. Next to your final death, which will be followed by the absolute healing of eternal life, this is the most absolute kind of healing. All other healings are partial. Something is sick and it has "died" a little, and the Father raises it back to life. But when you see somebody come back to life who was certifiably dead, it is a dramatic testimony to divine healing power.

The best scriptural example of this (besides Jesus Himself) is the story of the raising of Lazarus from the dead (see John 11:1-57). Modern-day resurrections confirm that this is still one of the kinds of healing that the Spirit of God can and will perform.

Yes, healing is the children's bread. It was in the days when Jesus walked on the earth and it still is the children's bread in these days when He lives in His body (that is you and me) as we live out our supernatural lives here on earth. As we press on, living a supernatural life, let us expect to see the fullness of the healing ministry of Jesus restored in our day.

Review

Healing is so basic and so vital to our supernatural life that Jesus calls it "the children's bread." Jesus modeled for us many different kinds of healing, and He expects us to carry on where He left off, activated in the spirit of Acts 10:38: "You know of Jesus of Nazareth, how God anointed Him with the Holy Spirit and with power, and how He went about doing good and healing all who were oppressed by the devil, for God was with Him" (*NASB*).

1. Why do we consider the natural healing process to be part of the healing that comes with the supernatural life? Who is the Author of all healing?

2. Review the primary types of healing. Which kinds of healing have you experienced personally? Can you testify about a particular healing?

3. In what way do you need healing today? Talk to God about it. Find out what He wants you do to.

Chapter 12

Finishing Well

At times, it can be very exciting to live a supernatural life, like living in a movie filled with special effects. But that's far from being the whole picture. As I have tried to make clear throughout this book, the supernatural life must encompass *all* of your life or it is not a life at all.

The quality of your supernatural life depends on how much you are growing to be like Jesus. The caliber of your personal character and vigor of your faith are all-important. Your ability to sustain loving relationships is also vital.

The supernatural life is mostly ordinary things—but with a difference. That difference is the life-giving Spirit of God who lives inside you and who "directs traffic." He will guide you, convict you and enable you. He will give meaning to everything. You will never be immune to difficulties, trials, disappointments, failures, slip-ups, problems or traumas, but He will see to it that even the worst experiences of your life will fit in with God's plan for your life.

Because of the Holy Spirit within you, you have everything you will need to live a successful supernatural life right up to when you arrive at death's door. Jesus saved you so that He could have you with Him eternally. His Spirit wants to make sure that you finish your race well.

When he reached the end of his earthly life, the apostle Paul, in spite of his prideful and violent start in life, and in spite of the firestorms he endured for the rest of his life, knew that he was finishing well. He wrote:

> I am already being poured out like a drink offering, and the time has come for my departure. I have fought the good fight, I have finished the race, I have kept the faith. Now there is in store for me the crown of righteousness, which the Lord, the righteous Judge, will award to me on that day—and not only to me, but also to all who have longed for his appearing (2 Tim. 4:6-8).

He had lived his life with his eye on the Lord Himself, who was holding his reward. He had been single-heartedly devoted to his Lord for decades, disregarding the opinions of others. From the moment he met Jesus on the road to Damascus, His life had been supernatural—and he had stayed the course.

The House that Is Built to Last

With this in mind, I want to tell you about a vivid dream I had.

I have noticed that revelatory dreams and supernatural encounters often carry a certain "feel" or atmosphere. This one was permeated with the presence of the jealousy of God. (The jealousy of God is His fierce zeal to have the undivided, devoted attention of His people.)

I was taken to a construction site where the foundation of a house was being prepared. Two angels came and stood at the front of each of the corners of the property, overseeing the construction process. The ground was rocky, and I had the strong sense that the area was earthquake-prone and that it had been shaken many times. I knew that it was going to be important to lay a good, deep foundation.

Very deep trenches were dug and cement trucks began to appear on the scene to pour the foundation. The first layer of cement was poured, and I watched as it set up. As it firmed up, writing in script appeared on the right front of the foundation. It read, "Jesus Christ, the Messiah of the Jew and the Gentile." I watched as script also appeared on the left front of the foundation. It read, "Apostles and prophets, fathers and mothers of the ages." It was as if the writing just rose to the surface and appeared. Of course I realized that this matches Ephesians 2:20, where God's household is "built on the foundation of the apostles and prophets, with Christ Jesus himself as the chief cornerstone."

The cement trucks pulled up again and another pouring proceeded. Script appeared on this second layer of the foundation as well. On the front right corner, the word "Humility" emerged, and on the left, it was "Integrity." The scene repeated a third time with a phrase surfacing on the freshly poured cement: "Intimate worship from a pure heart."

I was now keenly aware that this was no ordinary house that was being built. This was an apostolic house for the glory of God in the end times. Another cement truck came and unloaded its quick-drying substance. Once again words arose and appeared: "God's heart for the poor and the desperate." And as soon as those words rose to the top, another phrase popped into view, "God's healing presence." The foundation now appeared to be complete.

I was then awakened out of dreaming by hearing a clear word from the two angelic attendants who had been overseeing the construction of the house. The word I heard was, "The house that is built to last." Standing there in the jealousy of God, the angels had been positioned to oversee the construction, making sure that the foundation would be laid properly.

How Is Your House Being Built?

In the same way, I believe that the Holy Spirit is sending help to God's often-shaken people to make sure that the foundation of each of our personal lives is strong, secure and built to last. This is true as well for the corporate dwelling place of God—the Church—the Body of Christ.

Is your house founded on Jesus Christ, the Cornerstone (see 1 Pet. 2:6)? Is your house established upon the revelation, lifestyle and truths of the apostles and prophets—the fathers and mothers of the faith throughout the ages of the Church? Are you maintaining a life of integrity and humility with a heart filled with pure worship? Are you asking the Lord to restore the ancient foundation of God's heart for the poor and the desperate? Are you seeking the Lord for a greater release of His healing presence to demonstrate His love and mercy?

Since having this dream, I am asking myself these questions, and now I'm asking you: In the spirit of the jealousy of God, how is your house being built? When the winds and the rains and the storms come, is your house built to last (see Matt. 7:24-27)? *Is your house built to last?* God wants it to be well built. He wants it to last. He has claimed you for Himself.

Let us continue to acquire and apply wisdom from the Lord and build our houses so that they will stand firm as a testimony of His greatness. Let us inspect our houses—rather let us allow the Holy Spirit to conduct an inspection. Let us allow Him to correct insufficiencies in our house building. He will help you know if you are building your house on sand or on the solid rock.

Even if He seems to make you start over, it will be worth it. At times, I have felt that He came into my life and virtually jackhammered everything to pieces, only to take me deeper and reestablish it all better than before. Things that took me years to build, He has demolished, only to show me that those things were okay for that time, but because the gifts and callings of God are progressive in nature, they wouldn't have been strong enough or deep enough to support the kind of house that He wanted to build. It was as if I thought He was building a cottage when He wanted to build a skyscraper.

Together now, let's do a foundation check, considering seven signs of health in your earthly supernatural life. In chapter 5, we compared the North Star with a shooting star. Let's make sure that we are as fixed and well-oriented as North Stars, walking honestly toward our destination. At the end of the day, I want us each to be able to hear, "Well done, thou good and faithful servant" (see Matt. 25:21,23; Luke 19:17).

We can base our evaluation on Paul's words to the people of the church in Rome:

The hour has come for you to wake up from your slumber, because our salvation is nearer now than when we first believed. The night is nearly over; the day is almost here. So let us put aside the deeds of darkness and put on the armor of light. Let us behave decently, as in the daytime, not in orgies and drunkenness, not in sexual immorality and debauchery, not in dissension and jealousy. Rather, clothe yourselves with the Lord Jesus Christ, and do not think about how to gratify the desires of the sinful nature (Rom. 13:11-14).

Are you spiritually awake? Supernatural believers know what time it is. They know it is not a time to be "asleep at the switch." The darkness is approaching swiftly. The time is short. Soon it will be too late to respond to the Master's voice.

Is your life clean and holy? Have you "put aside the deeds of darkness"? Have you "put on the armor of light"? Supernatural believers have the ability to do just that. The "armor of light" keeps their lives clean and holy.

Are you seeking to extend His kingdom? Supernatural believers have a Kingdom mindset. Motivated to be involved in the work of the army of God to release the kingdom of God in their own place and time, they help extend the reach of the Kingdom. They know that they are under orders, and they fulfill their assignments.

Are you living a transparent, open and honest life? Most of the time, blatant sin is committed under the cover of darkness. When Paul says, "Let us behave decently, as in the daytime," we know what he means. Supernatural believers have nothing to hide. They're not lingering in the shadows to see how much they can get away with. They do not live by a double standard. It is refreshing to come across someone who is not fake in any way. Are you that kind of a person?

Are you avoiding carnal living? In the Scripture above, I think it is interesting that dissension and jealousy are listed right along with more overt sins such as sexual immorality and drunkenness.

Those hidden sins can apply to any of us—even as we undertake the process of evaluating our spiritual houses. Have you been comparing your house to someone else's, with some envy in your heart? Repent and ask God to help you rebuild your foundational identity in Him. Growth in holiness does not happen overnight. You have time to start fresh.

Are you leaning totally upon Jesus? To build your house well, you need to be intimately responsive to Him. You will, in the words of the passage above, clothe yourself "with the Lord Jesus Christ." Notice that you don't clothe yourself with only "Jesus Christ," but rather with "the *Lord* Jesus Christ." You put yourself under the authority and total *lordship* of Jesus, in every area of your life. This is what you signed up for. He's the One in charge. He's the One you are reflecting to the world. His is the reputation you are upholding.

Are you keeping your priorities right? This brings it back around. When it comes to sin, it's as if Paul is saying, "Don't even think about it." You know what will happen if you keep your eye on your Lord and you avoid the attractions of the world—the things that used to attract you will simply fade away. You'll starve out the devil; you'll crowd him out. Freed from his harassment, you can continue to build your house on its solid foundation.

A Word of Warning

Without the ongoing presence of the Holy Spirit, you will not be able to say yes to any of these questions. Sad to say, the history of the Church is littered with ruins of once-promising structures. You cannot build your spiritual house and maintain it well if you deny the Spirit whom you once invited to dwell in your heart. Those who fail to allow Him room will find that every one of these questions will be answered in the opposite way.

The moral of the story is clear—put on the Lord Jesus Christ, and keep Him on! You cannot grow past the wisdom of that statement.

Characteristics of a Supernatural People

Hermits will be limited in their expression of the school of the supernatural. You cannot be a supernatural person who is living a supernatural life unless you are somehow a part of a supernatural people who are serving God in unity and in some form of community.

Supernatural people are part of a *community of believers*. They are never isolated individuals. Together, they manifest an opposite spirit to the one that is in the world, living what I call "cross-current lives," by their lifestyle demonstrating that God is love. Correct doctrine is important, but Christianity is relational by its very nature, relational vertically (to God) and horizontally (toward others).

Another characteristic of supernatural people is that they are pioneers. They go forth, not by sight and their own logic and strength, but by *faith*. Abraham led his family away from their home without knowing where he was going (see Heb. 11:8-10). Sometimes we think that "walking in the supernatural" means that you will know everything ahead of time. Not so. Abraham is honored for his extreme faith. He is one of the fathers of our faith.

Supernatural people are *breakers for others*. What do I mean by that? According to Micah 2:13, there are those who go ahead and open the way for others. They pay the price as groundbreakers, so that other people can also enjoy God's presence and enter into His purposes. People who are living a supernatural life know that life is not just about "me, my and mine." They are willing to shoulder the task of opening the way for someone else.

These are people with a *message*. If you are a supernatural person, you carry a living word. A supernaturally natural Church becomes a prophetic message to the world, declaring that the cross of Jesus Christ is effective and that the Father loves His people. A supernatural Church does not speak only words of revelation or release—they are also living epistles, conveying the message of the Kingdom through their supernaturally natural lifestyle.

Supernatural Christians are a New Testament priesthood of believers with a passion for Jesus and compassion for people (see 1 Pet. 2:5,9). They will walk out their faith with corresponding actions of servanthood. They are a *relevant servant community*. Far more than those who perform random acts of kindness, they are part of a "conspiracy of kindness" (to borrow Steve Sjogren's term).

They are people with a *hearing ear and a seeing eye.* They have bought "eye salve" (see Rev. 3:18) to heal their blurred vision; they have been delivered from a deaf and dumb spirit that used to hinder their ability to hear the voice of Jesus. And they can bring others into the Body of Christ to participate in the same endeavor.

These are all characteristics of supernatural people. Are you one of them?

What *Would* Jesus Do?

Supernatural people ask themselves and each other, "What *would* Jesus do?" Filled with His Spirit, they can sense His nudges of direction or correction. His Word becomes clear. The guesswork is taken out of it.

Really what they are asking is "How would Jesus *be*?" Whatever He did and whatever He does is characterized by love and righteousness. Living in His light and finishing well involves contentment with whatever He sends our way. If you want to do what Jesus would do, you need to be filled with His love and let His righteousness work its way into your pores. Then you will be as contented as Paul was when he said:

> I have learned to be content in whatever circumstances I am. I know how to get along with humble means, and I also know how to live in prosperity; in any and every circumstance I have learned the secret of being filled and going hungry, both of having abundance and suffering need. I

can do all things through Him who strengthens
me (Phil. 4:11-13, *NASB*).

A contented spirit is the very opposite of a striving,
driving spirit. A contented believer does not try to find
peace and contentment in outward circumstances. (That
is always a recipe for *dis*content.) A contented believer has
allowed the supernatural power of God to infiltrate his or
her will and sense of purpose. A contented believer is living a supernatural lifestyle of unshakable trust in the
goodness of God and in His ongoing care for every one of
His own people.

Have you reached Paul's level of contentment? Not
many of us have. I know I haven't. I think my late wife did
reach it, early in her supernatural walk as a matter of fact.
She was content *not* to have a ministry. Her goal was not to
travel the world or to be an author or to found a humanitarian agency (all of which she did). Here is her goal, as she
wrote it in her last will and testament: "The goal of my life
is to love the Lord my God with all my heart, all the days of
my life." That meant that she was content wherever she
was. She was content wherever we lived. She was content
working in our crummy little barn, scooping up horse ma-
nure. She was content sitting in a rocking chair and doing
nothing. She was also content going on a great trip and
healing the sick. She knew that the pay was the same for
everyone, regardless of what the job is or how long they
work (see Matt. 20:1-16). That's true contentment!

How would Jesus *be*? Besides contented, He would be
righteous, and He enables us to be righteous too, if we
abide in Him:

Now, little children, abide in Him, so that when He appears, we may have confidence and not shrink away from Him in shame at His coming. If you know that He is righteous, you know that everyone also who practices righteousness is born of Him. . . . And everyone who has this hope fixed on Him purifies himself, just as He is pure (1 John 2:28,29; 3:3, *NASB*).

A person is able to live a supernatural life because that person fixes his or her eyes on Jesus. Whoever does this becomes pure. When you have your eyes fixed on Him, you love Him so much that you don't want your garments stained. You don't want them wrinkled. You want to be able to stand before Him on the final day, robed in righteousness (see Rev. 19:7-8).

What would Jesus do? What does He do all the time? He listens to the Father. He obeys Him. The Father is His reference point. In the same way, He needs to be ours.

When Jesus appeared to John the Beloved on the Isle of Patmos where the aged apostle had been exiled, He spoke of various churches that were in existence at the time, and each one has something in common with our situation today. To the church that had been established at Ephesus, he said:

You have persevered and have endured hardships for my name, and have not grown weary. Yet I hold this against you: You have forsaken your first love. Remember the height from which you have fallen! Repent and do the things you did at first. If you do not repent, I will come to you and remove your lampstand from its place (Rev. 2:3-5; see also Jer. 2:2 and Matt. 24:12).

Jesus would have us remember the fervor of our first love for Him. He would say to us, "Check your heart. Who is first in your affections? Is your love for Me deeper and stronger than ever?" And if we find that we, too, have forsaken our first love, we can turn back toward Him and reach out to Him. He has His arms out.

Love Never Fails

Love ties it all together. As we know from the very familiar lines of 1 Corinthians 13:

> If I speak in the tongues of men and of angels, but have not love, I am only a resounding gong or a clanging cymbal. If I have the gift of prophecy and can fathom all mysteries and all knowledge, and if I have a faith that can move mountains, but have not love, I am nothing. If I give all I possess to the poor and surrender my body to the flames, but have not love, I gain nothing. . . . And now these three remain: faith, hope and love. But the greatest of these is love (1 Cor. 13:1-3,13).

This Scripture came to life for the prophet Bob Jones on August 8, 1975, the day he died. He found himself in heaven with two lines of people. It seemed that about 98 percent of the people were in one long line and about 2 percent were in the other. He looked down and found that he was wearing a sparkling white robe (which was a big relief to him, because he had lived a life of sin in his early years).

But when he looked at the people in the longest line, he saw that they were clothed in whatever it was that they had loved most and whatever "god" they had been serving on their deathbeds. He could tell who had loved drugs or alcohol or sex. Those who had made money their god were wrapped in dollar bills.

There was a man dressed in white, and the people in the shorter line were drawing close to him, one by one. Bob found himself in this line. As he drew closer to the man dressed in white, he could see what was happening to the people in the other line—they were sliding down into a large dark place, never to return.

Bob turned his attention back to his line, which was the line for believers. As each one of them came to stand before him, the man dressed in white would ask only one short question: "Did you learn to love?" He would kiss them on the forehead and then the angels they had with them would go through a door with them.

When Bob's turn came, he was asked the same question. "Did you learn to love?" He knew that the man dressed in white could tell that he did. Bob Jones loved people. He wanted them to be saved. He loved souls. Then the man, who seemed like the Lord, asked him if he would return to earth for the sake of a billion unsaved souls, especially so that he could anoint some of the leaders who would be used to lead and nurture that many people. Bob said he would go back.

He found himself back in his body, alive on earth again. Ever since that time, he has been serving the Lord with all his heart, loving Him and other people. When it comes time for Bob to finish his course once and for all, he wants to finish well.

Living a Successful Supernatural Life

Along with Bob, let's live fully supernatural lives every day of our earthly lives. Then our translation into our heavenly life will be seamless. Let's surrender control over our lives and learn to sail with the wind of the Holy Spirit. With His loving help, we will make it!

Here you have it—my take on living a supernatural life—a life of adventure, a life of change, a life full of possibilities, a life where you expect to meet the unexpected at every turn, a life that is very natural, a life centered in Christ Jesus. A supernatural life is a life worth living! Can you think of any better way to live than the Holy Spirit-saturated, supernatural way?

Father, in Jesus' name, teach us how to live a successful supernatural Christian life. Teach us, Holy Spirit, how to be righteous, humble, obedient, clear-eyed and content in all things. Help us change in however we need to change so that we can reflect the character and gifts of Your Son. Fill us again with Your Holy Spirit so that we can finish well on this journey of a supernatural life with You. Amen.

Review

The supernatural life is like a seamless garment woven on the loom of God's love. Once you put it on, you need to take care of it so that it will last as long as you do. It can be cleaned and repaired as needed, but when the time comes for you to go Home, you will want to have it on so that you can exchange it for a pure white robe.

Stay close to the One who gave it to you so that at the end, you can finish well, having remained in love with the Giver of supernatural life right up until you draw your last breath on earth.

1. As you did your "building inspection" with the help of the Holy Spirit, what did He correct and amend? What did He commend?

2. If you were to die and go to heaven today, how would you answer the question, "Did you learn to love?"

3. Are you resolved to live a fully supernatural life all the days of your natural life? Who do you want to bring with you on this adventure?

Endnotes

Chapter 1: Yesterday, Today and Forever

1. This summary is based on Scriptures such as Luke 2:51; John 1:4-5,9; John 8:12; John 3:17; Luke 9:56; Matthew 16:23; Hebrews 4:15; Acts 10:38; Matthew 12:31-33; Luke 22:53; Philippians 2:7-8; John 5:19-30; John 14:30; John 8:47; Mark 15:16-32; 1 Corinthians 2:6-8; Hebrews 2:14-15; Colossians 1:13-14; Isaiah 53:3-6; 2 Corinthians 5:21; Hebrews 2:9; Revelation 22:14; Acts 2:32-35; Psalm 110:1-2; 1 Corinthians 15:20-28.

2. This summary of the effects of the cross is based on Scriptures such as John 6:57 and 10:30; Matthew 27:46; Isaiah 59:1-2; Habakkuk 1:13; Matthew 27:50; Leviticus 16:22; Psalm 16:8-11; Ephesians 4:9; Acts 2:25-31; 1 Peter 3:18-19; Psalm 71:20-21; Psalm 88; 1 Peter 3:18-19 and 4:6.

3. This summary of the life that Jesus exchanged for death is based on Scriptures such as Romans 6:23; 1 Corinthians 6:17; 1 John 1:3; Hebrews 13:5; Romans 8:11; 2 Corinthians 4:10-11; 1 Corinthians 15:51-54; 1 Thessalonians 4:17b; and Revelation 21:1-5.

Chapter 3: Filled and Overflowing

1. Example taken from Cindy Jacobs, *The Super-Natural Life: Experience the Power of God in Your Everyday Life* (Ventura, CA: Regal Books, 2005), p. 27.

2. As quoted in Jacobs, p. 26.

3. From Jack W. Hayford, *The Power and the Blessing: Celebrating the Disciplines of Spirit-Filled Living* (Colorado Springs, CO: Victor Books, 1994), p. 21. As quoted in Robert D. Heidler, *Experiencing the Spirit: Developing a Living Relationship with the Holy Spirit* (Ventura, CA: Regal Books, 1998), p. 35.

4. From Bill Bright, *The Holy Spirit: The Key to Supernatural Living* (San Bernardino, CA: Here's Life Publishers, Inc., 1980), pp. 116, 121. As quoted in Heidler, p. 35.

5. Charles Grandison Finney, *Memoirs* (New York: A.S. Barnes & Co., 1876), pp. 20-21.

Chapter 5: No Shortcuts

1. Andrew Murray, *Waiting on God* (New York: Cosmo Classics, 2007), Day 20, "Who Waits on Us," p. 100.

Chapter 6: Naturally Supernatural

1. William Cowper (1731–1800), "Light Shining Out of Darkness." Public domain.

2. See *Contagious Love International* (Munday Martin) at www.contagious loveintl.com.

Chapter 7: The Power of the Cross

1. Thayer and Smith, *The New Testament Greek Lexicon,* entry for *luo,* http://www.searchgodsword.org/lex/grk/view.cgi?number=3089.
2. Charles Haddon Spurgeon, *Twelve Sermons on Prayer* (London: Marshall, Morgan & Scott, n.d.), p. 50.

Chapter 8: Tools for Your Tool Belt

1. Based on Thayer and Smith, *The New Testament Greek Lexicon,* entry for *pistis,* http://www.searchgodsword.org/lex/grk/view.cgi?number=4102.
2. Based on Thayer and Smith, *The New Testament Greek Lexicon,* entry for *pisteuo,* http://www.searchgodsword.org/lex/grk/view.cgi?number=4100.

Chapter 9: Help Is on the Way!

1. James W. Goll, *The Beginner's Guide to Hearing God* (Ventura, CA: Regal, 2004, 2008), pp. 107-108. The subsequent 10 principles of divine guidance are also adapted from the same chapter of this book.
2. John Calvin, *Institutes of the Christian Religion,* trans. Henry Beveridge, vol. I (Edinburgh: T. & T. Clark, 1863), p. 145.
3. This line was quoted from a version of Psalm 104:4.
4. Much of what follows has been adapted from the book *God Encounters,* which I coauthored with my late wife, Michal Ann Goll (Shippensburg, PA: Destiny Image, 2005).

Chapter 11: The Children's Bread

1. Irenaeus, *Against Heresies,* book 2, chapter 32, section 4.
2. A. J. Gordon, *The Ministry of Healing* (Harrisburg, PA: Christian Publications, 1882, 1961), pp. 16-17.
3. A. B. Simpson, *The Gospel of Healing* (New York: Christian Alliance Pub. Co., 1915), pp. 15-17.
4. F. F. Bosworth, *Christ the Healer* (Grand Rapids, MI: Fleming H. Revell, 1975), p. 40.
5. T. L. Osborn, *Healing the Sick* (Tulsa, OK: OSFO Foundation, 1959), p. 151.
6. Hugh Jeter, *By His Stripes* (Springfield, MO: Gospel Publishing House, 1977), pp. 34-35.
7. John and Mark Sanford, *Deliverance and Inner Healing* (Grand Rapids, MI: Chosen Books, 1992), p. 50.

James W. Goll is a lover of Jesus who cofounded Encounters Network (based in Franklin, Tennessee), which is dedicated to changing lives and impacting nations by releasing God's presence through prophetic, intercessory and compassion ministry. James is the International Director of Prayer Storm, a 24/7/365 prayer media-based ministry. He is also the Director of the EN Alliance, a coalition of friends.

After pastoring in the Midwest, James was thrust into the role of itinerant teaching and training around the globe. He has traveled extensively to every continent, carrying a passion for Jesus wherever he goes. James desires to see the Body of Christ become the house of prayer for all nations and be empowered by the Holy Spirit to spread the good news to every nation and all peoples. He is the author of numerous books and training manuals as well as a contributing writer for several periodicals.

James is an instructor in the Wagner Leadership Institute and the Christian Leadership University and founded the God Encounters School of the Heart. He is a member of the Harvest International Ministry Apostolic Team and a consultant to several national and international ministries. James and Michal Ann Goll were married for more than 32 years before her graduation to heaven in the fall of 2008. They have four wonderful adult children, and James continues to make his home in the beautiful hills of Franklin, Tennessee.

Other Books by
James W. and Michal Ann Goll

God Encounters

Prayer Storm

Women on the Frontlines Series

Intercession

The Lost Art of Intercession

The Lost Art of Practicing His Presence

The Coming Israel Awakening

The Beginner's Guide to Hearing God

The Coming Prophetic Revolution

The Call of the Elijah Revolution

The Prophetic Intercessor

Shifting Shadows of Supernatural Experiences

The Seer

The Seer Devotional and Journal

James W. Goll 365 Day Personal Prayer Guide

Empowered Prayer

Empowered Women

Dream Language

Angelic Encounters

Adventures in the Prophetic

Praying for Israel's Destiny

Deliverance from Darkness

God's Supernatural Power in You

The Reformer's Pledge

*Discovering the Seer in You, Exploring the Gift and Nature
of Dreams, Prayer Storm and many other study guides,
CD albums and DVD messages.*

For more information:

James W. Goll
Encounters Network
P.O. Box 1653
Franklin, TN 37065

visit: www.encountersnetwork.com
www.prayerstorm.com
www.compassionacts.com
email: info@encountersnetwork.com

Also Available in the Beginner's Guide Series

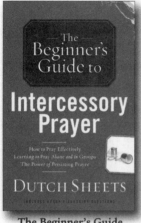

**The Beginner's Guide
to Intercessory Prayer**
Dutch Sheets
ISBN 978.08307.45395

**The Beginner's Guide
to Hearing God**
James W. Goll
ISBN 978.08307.46118

**The Beginner's Guide to
the Gift of Prophecy**
Jack Deere
ISBN 978.08307.46026

**The Beginner's Guide to
Spiritual Warfare**
Neil T. Anderson & Timothy Warner
ISBN 978.08307.46019